Easy Street

Name _____

Easy does it! What is each house worth? Count the money in each house on Easy Street. Write the amount on the line.

Example

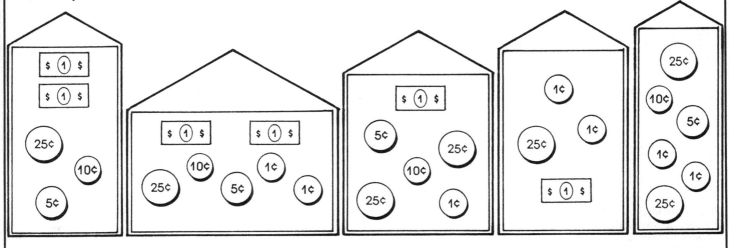

$2.40   _____   _____   _____   _____

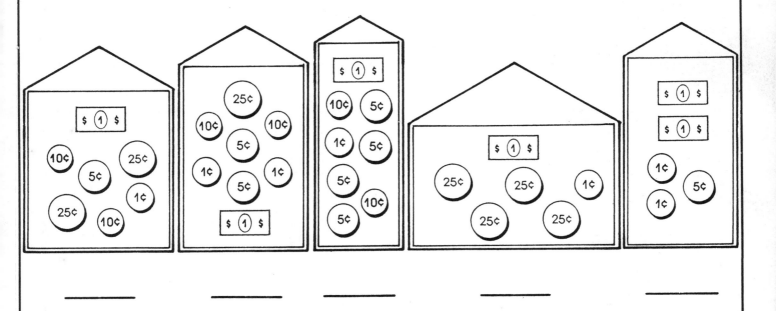

_____   _____   _____   _____   _____

Your Answer's SAFE with Me

Name _____

Find the right "combination" to open each safe. Draw the bills and coins needed to make each amount.

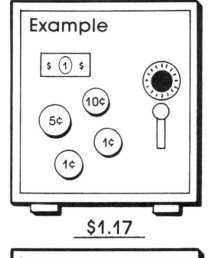

Example

$1.17

$2.04

$1.79

$2.46

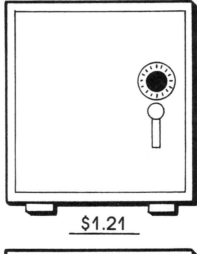

$1.21

$3.10

$1.39

$2.16

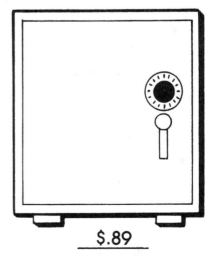

$.89

IF8746 Math Topics

Coupon Capers

Name _____

Cut the cost with these coupons. Subtract the cents off from the price. How much do the books cost now?

Example

Work Space

$1.87
$.58 OFF

$1.\overset{7\,1}{8}7$
$-\ .58$
———
$1.29

New Cost   _$1.29_

$2.06
$.37 OFF

New Cost _____

$1.00
$.25 OFF

New Cost _____

$3.15
$.86 OFF

New Cost _____

$2.54
$1.17 OFF

New Cost _____

$4.61
$2.18 OFF

New Cost _____

$1.62
$.44 OFF

New Cost _____

$5.31
$2.16 OFF

New Cost _____

$2.01
$.74 OFF

New Cost _____

$4.83
$1.79 OFF

New Cost _____

$6.35
$1.27 OFF

New Cost _____

$3.28
$.96 OFF

New Cost _____

IF8746 Math Topics

Top "Billing"

Name _____

The spotlight is on you!

Circle the amount you would give the clerk to buy each hat.

Then subtract to find how much change you would get.

Example

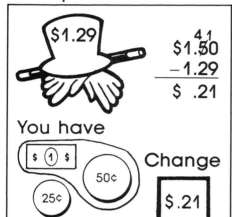

$$\begin{array}{r} 4\,1 \\ \$1.\cancel{50} \\ -1.29 \\ \hline \$\ .21 \end{array}$$

You have

Change

$.21

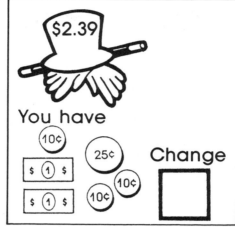

You have

Change

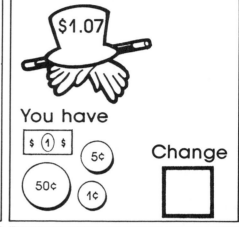

You have

Change

You have

Change

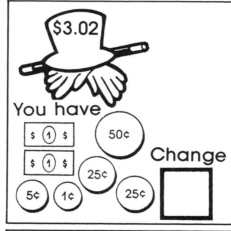

You have

Change

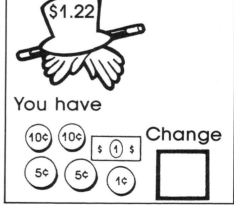

You have

Change

You have

Change

You have

Change

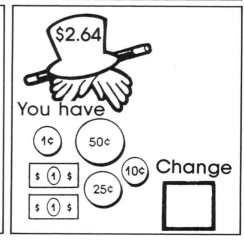

You have

Change

IF8746 Math Topics

Wordsworth Worm

Name _____

What are these words worth?
Write the amount of each letter. Add.

N	$.37
O	$.44
P	$.17
R	$.25
S	$.69
T	$.36
Y	$.71
M	$.33
L	$.54
I	$.84
H	$.52
G	$.28
E	$.77
D	$.49
C	$.59
B	$.43
A	$.68

Example

M	$.33
O	$.44
N	$.37
E	$.77
Y	+ $.71
	$2.62

CANDY +_____

GAMES +_____

GHOST +_____

SHAPE +_____

OPENS +_____

MAGIC +_____

SPEND +_____

PLAID +_____

DOLLAR +_____

CENTS +_____

BRAND +_____

SPORT +_____

DIMES +_____

EARNS +_____

CHANGE +_____

IF8746 Math Topics

Pizza "Dough" Business!

Name _____

The number of pieces tells you how many coins to use. Write in the amounts to equal the total price of these pizzas.

Example

$.25

$.25

$.25

$.10

total price
$.85

total price
$1.81

total price
$2.00

total price
$.74

total price
$.90

total price
$.85

total price
$.87

total price
$1.26

total price
$1.51

IF8746 Math Topics

One-Stop Shopping

Skill: 2-step problems with money (adding, subtracting)

Name _____

Stash McCash is shopping! Find the total cost of the items. Then find how much change Stash should receive.

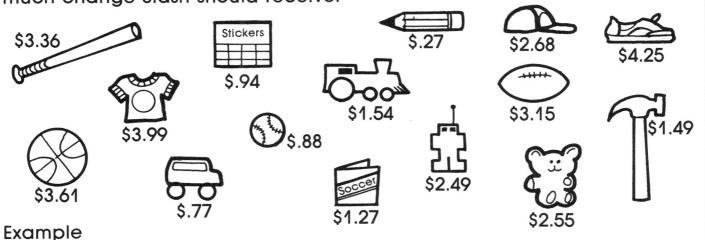

$3.36   Stickers $.94 $.27 $2.68 $4.25

$3.99 $.88 $1.54 $3.15 $1.49

$3.61 $.77   Soccer $1.27 $2.49 $2.55

Example

Stash has $5.00 Buys	Stash has $8.50 Buys	Stash has $7.04 Buys	Stash has $9.00 Buys

Box 1 (Example):
Stash has $5.00
Buys

 .88
 .77
 +1.54
3.19

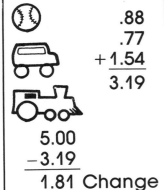

5.00
−3.19
1.81 Change

Box 2:
Stash has $8.50
Buys

Change

Box 3:
Stash has $7.04
Buys

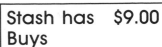
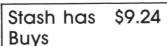
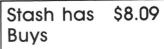

Change

Box 4:
Stash has $9.00
Buys

Change

Box 5:
Stash has $10.95
Buys

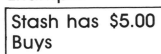

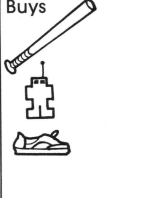

Change

Box 6:
Stash has $10.00
Buys

Change

Box 7:
Stash has $9.24
Buys

Change

Box 8:
Stash has $8.09
Buys

Change

IF8746 Math Topics

Dialing for Dollars

Name _____

Write the amount of money each number stands for. Add to get the total amount.

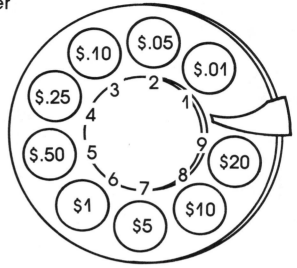

Example

Phone Number 231-6411	Phone Number 331-7842
$ .05	_____
.10	_____
.01	_____
$1.00	_____
.25	_____
.01	_____
+ .01	+ _____
$1.43	

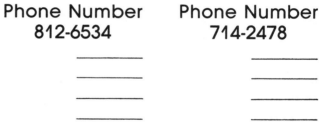

Phone Number 415-9336	Phone Number 513-8662	Phone Number 812-6534	Phone Number 714-2478
_____	_____	_____	_____
_____	_____	_____	_____
_____	_____	_____	_____
_____	_____	_____	_____
_____	_____	_____	_____
_____	_____	_____	_____
+ _____	+ _____	+ _____	+ _____

Phone Number 611-4933	Phone Number 235-6217	Phone Number 731-2566	Phone Number 692-3471
_____	_____	_____	_____
_____	_____	_____	_____
_____	_____	_____	_____
_____	_____	_____	_____
_____	_____	_____	_____
+ _____	+ _____	+ _____	+ _____

What a Great Catch!

Name _____

This is "fishy" business! Use your money "sense" to solve these problems.

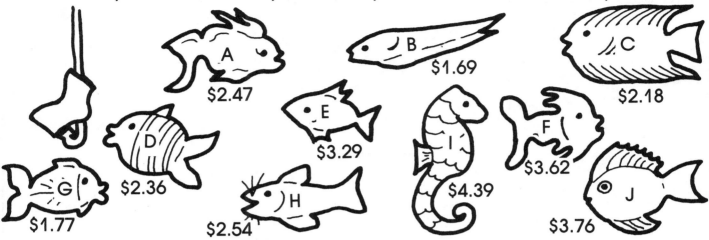

$2.47 (A)	$1.69 (B)
$2.18 (C)	$3.29 (E)
$2.36 (D)	$3.62 (F)
$1.77 (G)	$4.39 (I)
$2.54 (H)	$3.76 (J)

Buy fish	$2.47
A, C and H.	2.18
	+2.54
Total Cost	$7.19

You have $4.00.
Buy fish D.
How much money
is left?

You have $10.00.
Buy fish E and J.
How much money
is left?

Buy 4 of fish I.

Total Cost

You have $5.75
Buy fish G and C.

How much money
is left?

Buy fish
D, F, J and B.

Total Cost

Buy 6 of fish E.

Total Cost

Buy 3 of fish J
and 6 of fish D.

Total Cost

You have $10.76
Buy 3 of fish A.

How much money
is left?

         IF8746 Math Topics

Money Monsters

Name _____

Put X's in the boxes next to each Money Monster to show how many bills and coins are needed to equal the price of each monster.

		$10.00	$5.00	$1.00	$.50	$.25	$.10	$.05	$.01
Example	$12.47	X		X X		X	X X		X X
	$14.59								
	$20.31								
	$16.84								
	$32.55								
	$41.77								
	$39.16								
	$27.94								

Half-Time

Name _____

Great football players need good "timing"! Write the times on the footballs. Write another way to say the time on the line.

Example

10:30

Half past 10

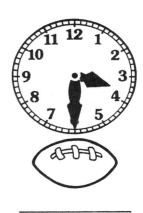

_____

_____

_____

_____

_____

_____

_____

_____

_____

_____

_____

Time to Tune In

Name _____

Get "in tune" with time. Give the time on these jam boxes by drawing the hands and filling in the blank lines.

Example

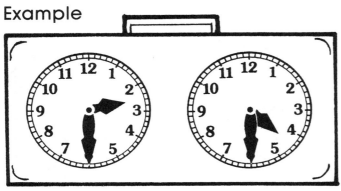

2 hours later
than 2:30   ___4:30___

3 hours earlier
than 2:00   _____

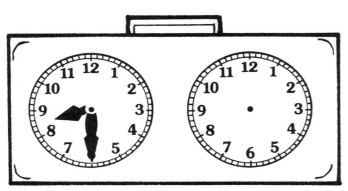

4 hours later
than 8:30   _____

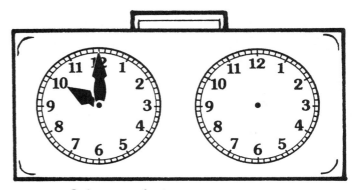

2 hours later
than 10:00   _____

5 hours earlier
than 1:30   _____

3 hours earlier
than 7:30   _____

Missing Hands

Name _____

The minute hands are missing on these clocks. Can you still tell what hour or half-hour the clocks show? Write the time on the line and draw the missing minute hand.

(Hint: If the time is exactly on the hour, then the hour hand is exactly on the number. If the time is on the half-hour, then the minute hand is half way between the numbers.)

Example

9:30   _____   _____   _____

_____   _____   _____   _____

_____   _____   _____   _____

_____   _____   _____   _____

Pizza Time

Name _____

Chef "Time-It-Right" is baking pizzas. Can you help him fill in his timing schedule?

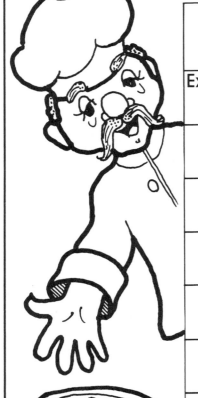

In the Oven	Baking Time	Out of the Oven
Example 6:00	1/2 hour	6:30
8:30	2 hours	
4:30	1 hour	
9:00		10:00
1:30	2 1/2 hours	
5:00		6:30
	1 hour	4:00
12:00	2 1/2 hours	
	1/2 hour	7:30
8:00		9:30
2:30	1 1/2 hours	
	3 hours	2:00
3:30		5:00

Solar Scholars

Name _____

Keep your sunny side up! Write the time.

Example

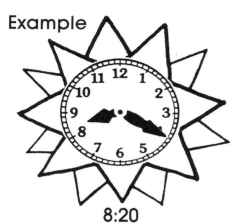

8:20

_____

_____

_____

_____

_____

_____

_____

_____

_____

_____

_____

Time On My Hands

Name _____

Draw the hour and minute hands.

Example

3:35

10:05

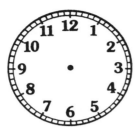

4:55

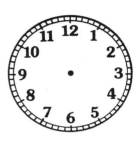

8:10

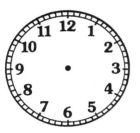

12:50

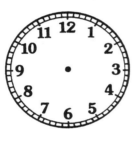

9:20

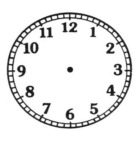

7:25

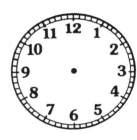

1:15

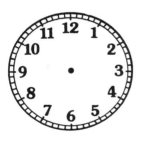

11:45

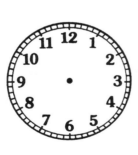

3:30

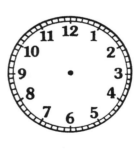

6:40

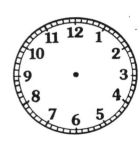

12:55

2:00

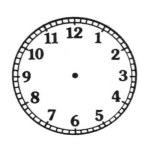

5:35

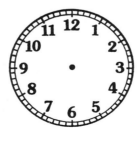

3:15

10:50

IF8746 Math Topics

Father Time Teasers

Name _____

Father Time doesn't want to tease you with these. He just wants you to work a little harder to figure out: "What time was it?" or "What time will it be?"

Example

25 minutes ago
5:35
_____

10 minutes later
_____

40 minutes ago
_____

35 minutes ago
_____

50 minutes later
_____

15 minutes ago
_____

20 minutes later
_____

45 minutes ago
_____

5 minutes ago
_____

30 minutes later
_____

55 minutes later
_____

25 minutes ago
_____

Let the Good "Times" Roll

Name _____

It's skating "time"! Fill in the chart for these skaters.

	Began Skating	Skating Time	Finished Skating
Tim	Example 5:15	45 minutes	6:00
Brent		20 minutes	3:15
Megan	8:10		9:15
Michelle		1 hour and 10 minutes	4:20
Josh	7:40	55 minutes	
Matt	3:05		5:30
Sue		1 hour and 40 minutes	7:00
Greg	1:25	35 minutes	
Sarah	12:30		1:45
Barb		25 minutes	12:00
Pat	4:50		6:00
Lisa	10:35	1 hour and 10 minutes	
Chad		50 minutes	8:20

It's About Time!

Name _____

Write the letter of the card that matches the clock on the line under the clock.

Example

____H____

_____

_____

_____

_____

_____

_____

_____

_____

_____

A	B	C	D	E
4:05	5:40	11:10	10:15	8:25

F	G	H	I	J
12:55	5:20	2:50	3:20	1:45

60 Minutes

Name _____

Give the time to the exact minute.

Example

12:17

_____

_____

_____

_____

_____

_____

_____

_____

_____

_____

_____

_____

_____

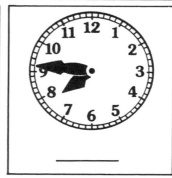

_____

_____

IF8746 Math Topics

Minute Men

Name _____

Add the clock hands to these "Minute Men" clocks.

Example

4:42

9:03

6:51

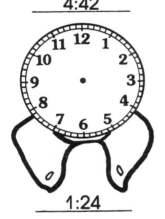

1:24

7:33

10:11

3:58

12:01

2:49

4:17

5:36

8:23

 IF8746 Math Topics

Skill: Figuring elapsed time

A "Shapely" Time Line

Name ______________________________

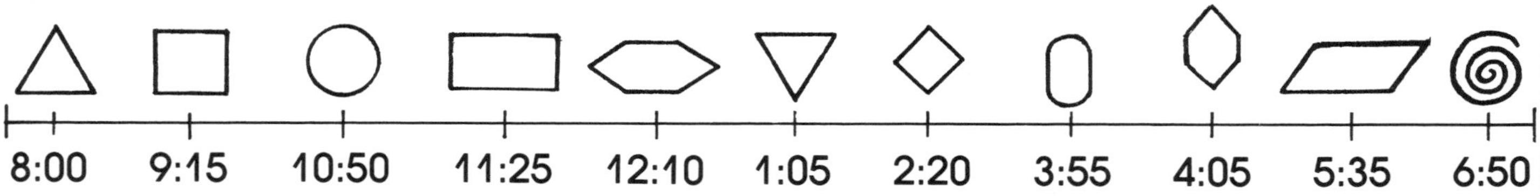

8:00
9:15
10:50
11:25
12:10
1:05
2:20
3:55
4:05
5:35
6:50

Let's "shape up" on time! Use this time line to tell how much time has passed between the following shapes.

Example

1.
to

9:15 to 11:25

2 hrs. 10 min.

2.
to

______ to ______

____

3.
to

______ to ______

____

4.
to

______ to ______

____

5.
to

______ to ______

____

6.
to

______ to ______

____

7.
to

______ to ______

____

8.
to

______ to ______

____

9.
to

______ to ______

____

10.
to

______ to ______

____

11.
to

______ to ______

____

12.
to

______ to ______

____

13.
to

______ to ______

____

14.
to

______ to ______

____

15.
to

______ to ______

____

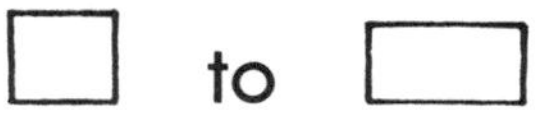

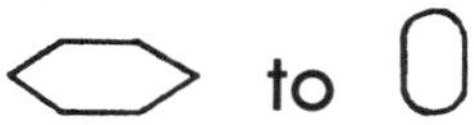

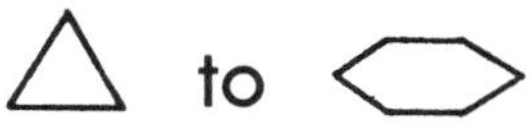

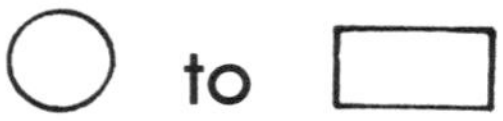

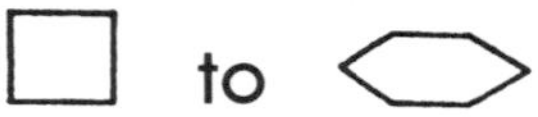

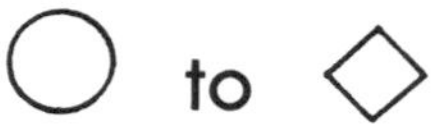

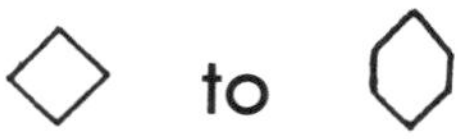

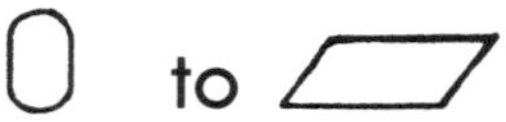

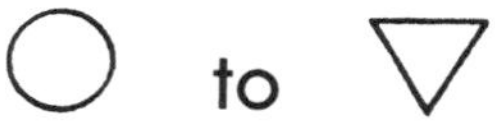

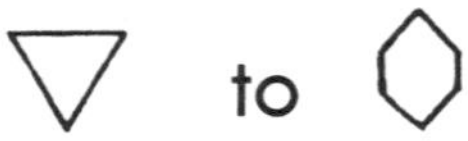

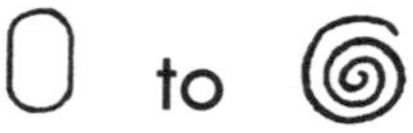

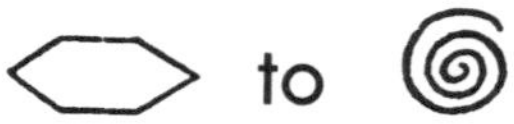

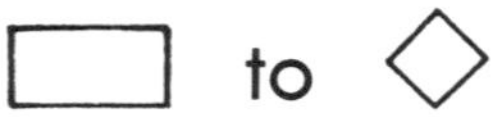

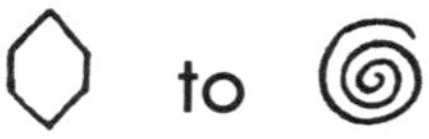

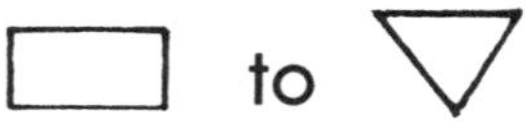

Time "Tables"

Name _____

"Set" these tables by drawing the hands on these clocks.

Example

10 minutes **before**

12:17

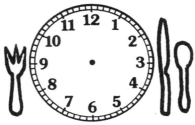

36 minutes **after**

8:19

8 minutes **before**

1:05

21 minutes **after**

8:40

16 minutes **before**

4:30

46 minutes **after**

10:11

32 minutes **before**

5:25

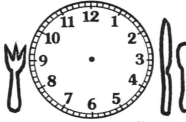

11 minutes **after**

3:16

24 minutes **before**

12:30

17 minutes **after**

1:31

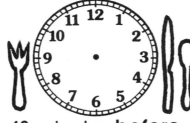

43 minutes **before**

2:01

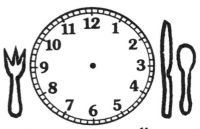

18 minutes **after**

6:45

IF8746 Math Topics

Matching Minutes

Name _____

Match these minutes by drawing lines from the clock to the digital time, then to the correct words.

Example

• 3:36 •

• four minutes before two o'clock

• 1:56 •

• seventeen minutes before nine o'clock

• 8:43 •

• two minutes after five o'clock

• 9:41 •

• nineteen minutes before ten o'clock

• 5:02 •

• twenty-four minutes before four o'clock

Minute Maid!

Name _____

How long does it take the "Minute Maid" to do her household tasks?

	Time Started	Length of Task	Time Ended
Polishing	Example 9:14	35 minutes	9:49
Dusting		42 minutes	8:00
Waxing	10:03		10:51
Mopping	2:36	29 minutes	
Cleaning Windows	4:45		5:32
Serving Breakfast		18 minutes	7:30
Laundry	11:10	58 minutes	
Ironing	12:13		1:00
Serving Lunch	11:30	24 minutes	
Vacuuming		41 minutes	3:57
Serving Dinner	5:30		5:57
Hanging Curtains	6:26	56 minutes	
Making Beds	8:03		8:41

It's High-Time!

Name _____

A.M. is the time after 12:00 midnight and before 12:00 noon.
P.M. is the time after 12:00 noon and before 12:00 midnight.
Write **A.M.** or **P.M.** for these events.

Example

1. The sun sets. __P.M.__

2. You get up. _____

3. You eat dinner. _____

4. Afternoon _____

5. The sun rises. _____

6. Morning cartoons _____

7. You have lunch. _____

8. Evening _____

9. Afternoon soccer _____

10. You eat breakfast. _____

11. Morning exercises _____

12. Evening TV shows _____

13. Evening piano class _____

14. Morning music class _____

15. Home from school _____

16. Afternoon art class _____

17. Catch morning bus _____

18. After-school snack _____

19. You go to bed. _____

20. Morning gym _____

21. Before school jobs _____

22. Evening dance class _____

23. Afternoon reading _____

24. Morning snack _____

Take Time for These . . .

Name _____

Be right on time! Write the exact time shown on these clocks.

Example

_____ 6:47 _____   _____   _____   _____

_____   _____   _____   _____

_____   _____   _____   _____

_____   _____   _____   _____

Minute Monsters

Name _____

The Minute Monsters have their pairs of shoes mixed up. Cut out the shoes. Glue the matching pairs onto another paper.

 1 hr. 15 min. after 6:20

 6:50

 2 hrs. 5 min. after 1:10

 8:00

 45 min. after 2:35

 8:20

 2 hrs. 10 min. before 4:00

 7:35

 3 hrs. 10 min. before 10:00

 2:20

 1 hr. 50 min. before 6:10

 2:30

 45 min. after 1:45

 4:20

 55 min. before 3:15

 3:45

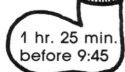 1 hr. 25 min. before 9:45

 1:50

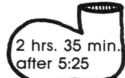 2 hrs. 35 min. after 5:25

 3:15

 1 hr. 10 min. before 12:00

 3:20

 3 hrs. 15 min. before 7:00

10:50

Just Like Clockwork!

Name _____

Use your time wisely. Draw the hands on these clocks to show the times given.

Example

5:14

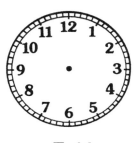

7:46

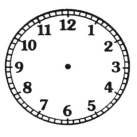

1:22

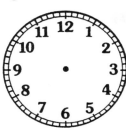

10:32

8:54

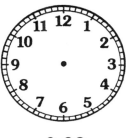

3:02

9:41

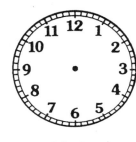

12:24

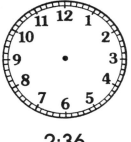

2:36

4:19

11:57

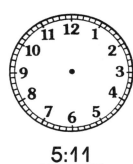

5:11

6:08

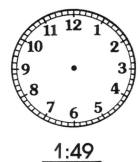

1:49

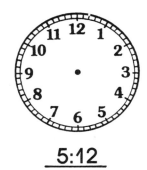

5:12

8:38

Tim's Time Line

Name _____

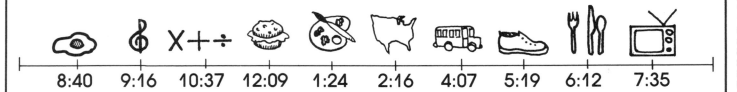

8:40   9:16   10:37   12:09   1:24   2:16   4:07   5:19   6:12   7:35

The time line shows the times that Tim does these things each school day. How much time passes between these events? It's "TIME" to begin!

Example

---

1. How long from  until 🗺 ?

12:09 to 2:16 = 2 hrs. 7 min.

---

5. How long between 👟 and 🍴 ?

_____ to _____ = _____

---

2. How long between 🍳 and  ?

_____ to _____ = _____

---

6. How long between X+÷ class and 🎨 ?

_____ to _____ = _____

---

3. How long from 🗺 class to 🚌 ?

_____ to _____ = _____

---

7. How long from 🚌 to 📺 ?

_____ to _____ = _____

---

4. How long between ♪ class and X+÷ class?

_____ to _____ = _____

SUPER CHALLENGE!
8. How long from the beginning to the end of Tim's Time Line?

_____ to _____ = _____

---

*Bonus – Make your own time line for **your** school day.
Make up questions for a friend to answer. Have a good "TIME"!

Measurement . . .

Name _____

SUITS ME TO A TEE!
How many centimeters from the tee to the flag? Stay on "course"!

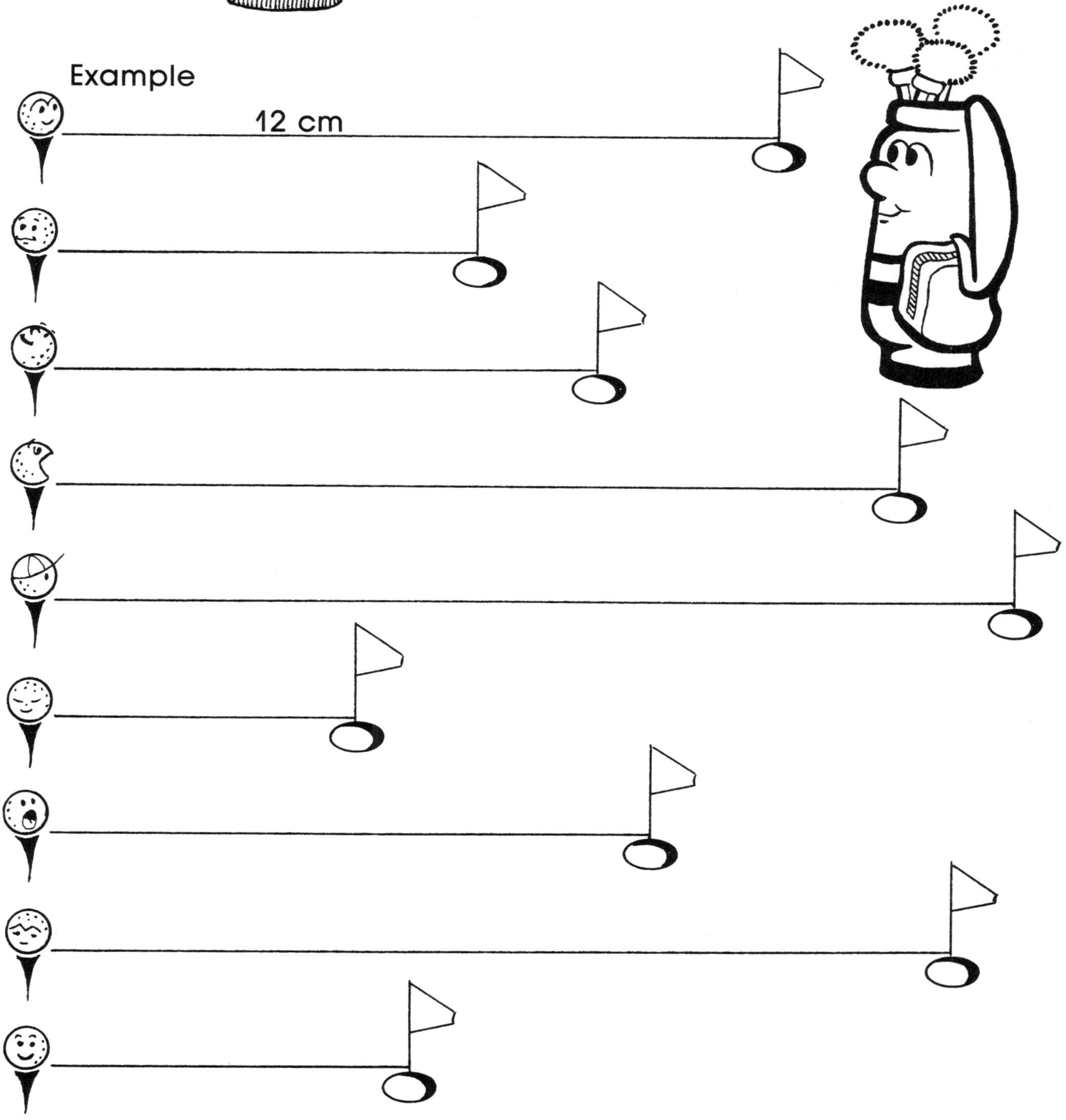

Example

12 cm

Batter Up!

Name _____

1. How many centimeters from home plate to first base? _____

2. The ball in left field is _____ from the pitcher's mound. Measure from ★.

3. How far is it from the pitcher's mound to home plate? _____
Measure from ★.

4. The ball in right field is _____ from home plate.
Measure from ★.

5. A throw from third base to first base would be _____ long.

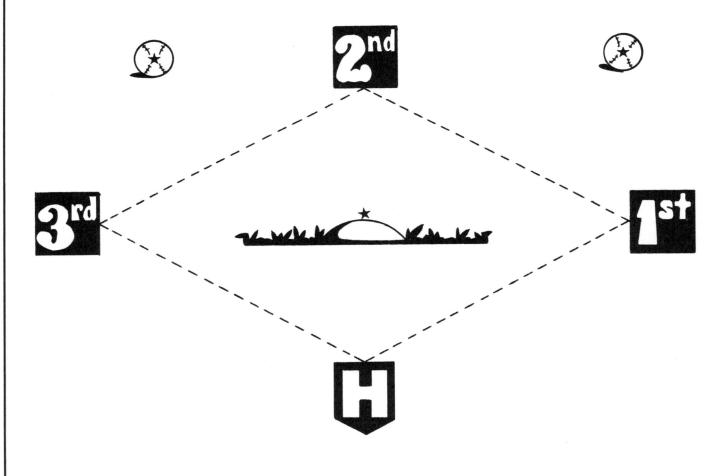

Sawing Logs

Name _____

Measure the logs to the nearest centimeter.

Example

 __8 cm__

 _____

 _____

 _____

 _____

 _____

 _____

Luck of
the Draw!

Name _____

1. In Box A, draw a pencil that is 15 cm long (from the widest part of the eraser to the pencil point). The pencil is 2 cm wide. Color and write your name on it.

2. In Box B, draw a rectangle that is 7 cm long and 4 cm wide. Decorate it as a birthday present.

3. In Box C, draw a triangle with all three sides 4 cm long. Put a point toward the top and make it into a funny car.

Box A

Box B

Box C

The Metric Kingdom

Name _____

Visit the Metric Amusement Park by measuring the distance to these attractions. Measure from ★ to ★.

1. The Fantastic Ferris Wheel is _____ cm from Dandy's Dart Booth.

2. The beach ball is _____ cm from Barney, the Balloon Man.

3. The Centimeter Streak Roller Coaster is _____ cm from the Fantastic Ferris Wheel.

4. The antique car is _____ cm from Barney, the Balloon Man.

5. The Centimeter Sailor Sailboat is _____ cm from the roller coaster.

6. Dandy's Dart Booth is _____ cm from Gram's Bell Ringer Booth.

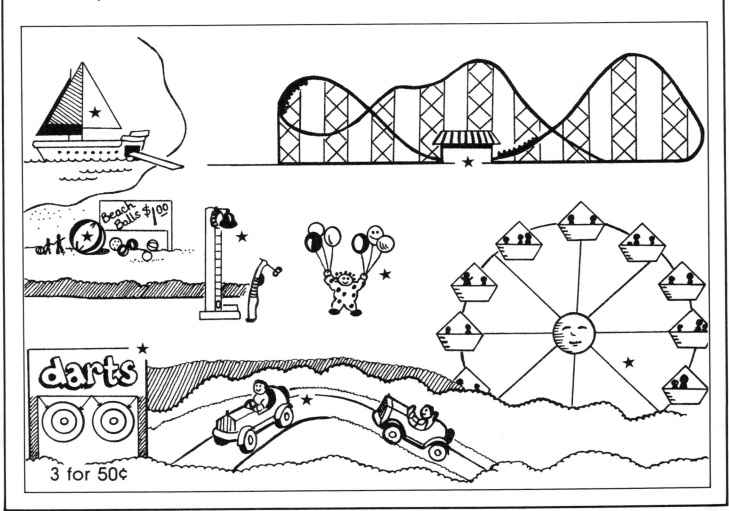

IF8746 Math Topics

Ella Elephant

Name _____

Read the picture graph. Answer the questions.

Monday
Tuesday
Wednesday
Thursday
Friday

1. How many butterflies did Ella Elephant catch on
   Monday?____ Tuesday?____ Wednesday?____ Thursday?____
   Friday____?
2. On what day did she catch the most?_____
   Color them blue.
3. On what day did she catch the least?_____
   Color them red.
4. How many butterflies did Ella catch in all? _____
5. Draw a green ▢ around the best day to catch
   butterflies.

 IF8746 Math Topics

Flower Graph

Name _____

Cut out and match the flowers to the graph.

Daisies					
Sunflowers					
Tulips					
Roses					

How many tulips? ____ Sunflowers? ____ Roses? ____ Daisies? ____
How many more tulips than roses? ____
How many more daisies than sunflowers? ____
How many sunflowers and tulips? ____
How many roses and daisies? ____

IF8746 Math Topics

Potato Face

Name _____

Read the line graphs to draw the potato faces.

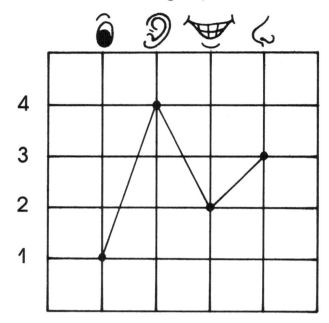

How many?

👁️'s _____ 👂's _____ 😬's _____ 👃's _____

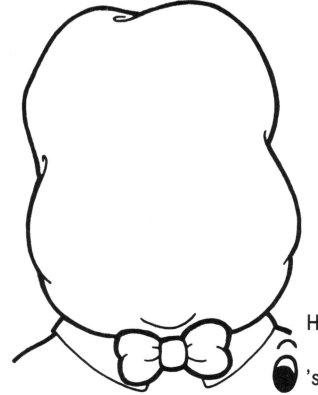

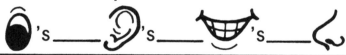

How many?

👁️'s _____ 👂's _____ 😬's _____ 👃's _____

Frog Bubbles

Name _____

Color the picture.

Finish the line graph to show how many bubbles.

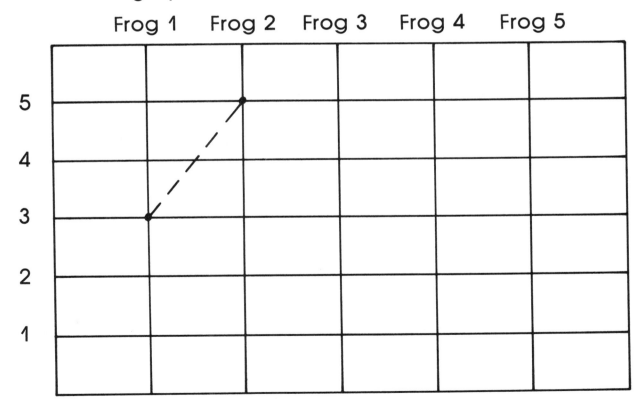

How many bubbles? Frog 1? ____ 2? ____ 3? ____ 4? ____ 5? ____
Which frog blew the most bubbles? ____ Which frog blew the
least? ____

Lizzy the Lizard

Name _____

Lizzy the Lizard has a great collection of insects. She is always on the lookout for new and different types of bugs.

1. Lizzy collected 5 ants and 6 beetles in a morning. What was the sum?

2. Lizzy the Lizard caught 11 crickets and 7 grasshoppers in an evening. How many insects did she catch in all?

3. Lizzy found 7 bees and 8 wasps on a tour of her garden. How many insects did she find?

4. Lizzy and her brother Dizzy found 7 stinkbugs and 6 lice on Sunday. How many insects did they find altogether?

5. Lizzy caught 7 mud wasps. Izzy caught 6 waterbugs. Dizzy caught 4 flies. How many bugs did they catch in all?

6. Lizzy found 9 ants in the morning and 9 more ants in afternoon. How many ants did she find in all?

Suzy D. Spider

Name _____

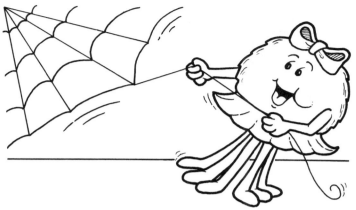

1. Suzy D. Spider has 8 legs. Her friend Ant Betty has 6 legs. How many more legs does Suzy have?

2. Suzy caught 16 flies in a week. The next week she caught only 9 flies. What was the difference?

3. Suzy had 15 children. 9 of them were boys. How many were girls?

4. Suzy scared 11 people on Sunday. She scared only 6 people on Monday. What was the difference?

5. Suzy is 16 millimeters long. Her sister is 11 millimeters long. How much longer is Suzy?

6. Suzy trapped 17 flies in her web. Her sister Sally trapped 8 flies. How many more did Suzy trap?

7. Suzy D. Spider ate 12 mealworms and 18 fruit flies in a week. How many more fruit flies did she eat?

The Missing Teeth

Name _____

1. Cal Coyote had 42 teeth. He lost 11 teeth. How many does he have left?

2. Roger Raccoon had 40 teeth before 10 fell out. How many does he have left?

3. Harry House Mouse used to have 16 teeth. He now has 11 teeth. How many of his teeth has he lost?

4. Red Fox has 31 teeth now. He used to have 42 teeth. How many did he lose?

5. Peter Possum used to have 50 teeth. The busy tooth fairy has paid him for 40 teeth. How many teeth does Peter have left?

6. Stinky the Skunk has 12 teeth. He used to have 34. How many of his teeth has he lost?

7. Woody Woodchuck now has 11 teeth. He used to have 22 teeth. How many has he lost?

McMealworm

Name _____

McMealworm's is the latest restaurant of that famous fast food creator, Buggs I. Lyke. His McMealworm Burger costs $1.69. An order of Roasted Roaches costs $.59 for the regular size and $.79 for the large size. A Cricket Cola is $.89.

1. You buy a McMealworm Burger and a regular order of Roasted Roaches. What is the total?

2. Your best friend in class orders a McMealworm Burger, a large order of Roasted Roaches and a Cricket Cola. How much will it cost?

3. Your teacher buys a Cricket Cola and a regular order of Roasted Roaches. What does it cost?

4. The principal is very hungry, so his bill comes to $14.37. How much change will he get from $20.00?

5. Your mom goes to McMealworm's to buy your dinner. She spends $3.37. How much change does she get from a $5.00 bill?

6. You have $1.17 in your bank. How much more do you need to pay for a McMealworm Burger?

Wacky Waldo's Animal Circus

Name _____

Wacky Waldo has trained a very unusual animal circus. He has taught sharks to ride tricycles. He has trained mice to scare tigers and snakes to be as cuddly as kittens. He has even trained donkeys to fly like sparrows.

1. Wacky Waldo taught 15 sharks to ride tricycles and 34 mice to scare tigers. How many more mice has he taught?

2. Waldo trained 17 donkeys to fly through the air like little birds. He also taught 18 snakes to cuddle up like little kittens. How many animals were trained altogether?

3. Waldo had trained 45 flying donkeys. One night, 26 donkeys flew away. How many donkeys were left?

4. Wacky has 112 flies who have been taught to bite fish and 98 flies who have been taught to chase frogs. What is the total?

5. One evening, 69 sharks rode tricycles. On the same night, 46 whales rode bicycles. How many animals were riding that night?

6. On Sunday, 56 snakes learned to be warm and cuddly. On Monday, 38 more snakes learned how to cuddle up. How many more snakes were trained on Sunday?

Percy P. Porcupine

Name _____

Percy P. Porcupine created a sensation one morning when he decided to go to school to get an education.

To School

1. Percy met 19 dogs and 12 cats on the way to school, but none of them wanted to play with him. How many animals did he meet?

2. Percy had a disagreement with the school bully. The bully got 64 quills in his right hand and 56 in his left. How many more quills were in his right hand?

3. A kindergarten teacher thought Percy was cute and tried to pet him. She got 37 quills stuck in her hand. She got 18 out. How many were still in her hand?

4. Percy visited the third grade classroom and counted 16 boys and 17 girls. What was the sum?

5. A dog named Bow-Wow tried to rub noses with Percy. He got 27 quills in his nose and 16 in his neck. How many quills did he get in all?

6. Percy visited the principal. He gave him 26 quills. He gave the secretary 35 quills. How many more quills did the secretary get?

 IF8746 Math Topics

Beetle in a Box

Name _____

A brand-new fast food place called **Beetle in a Box** has opened up near your school. You can buy a Beetle Burger for $1.39, Fried Flies for $.79 and a Cocoon Cola for $.98.

1. You order a Beetle Burger and a Cocoon Cola on your way home from school. How much will they cost?

2. Your teacher wants a snack after school. She orders Fried Flies and a Cocoon Cola. What is the total?

3. You and your family had dinner at **Beetle in a Box**. The bill was $15.78. Your father gave the waitress a $20.00 bill. How much change should he have received?

4. Jamie gave the owner a $10.00 bill to pay for an order that cost $4.14. How much change did he get?

5. How much will it cost you for a Beetle Burger and Fried Flies?

6. The nearest hamburger stand sells beef burgers for $1.88. How much less is a Beetle Burger?

Mean Monster's Multiplication

Name _____

Mean Monster is a football player for the Oki Doki Outlaws. He weighs over 400 pounds and is 7 feet tall. He is not a good student. He spent 3 years in first grade. He thinks there are only 24 letters in the alphabet because he thinks **P's** and **B's** are something to eat.

1. Mean Monster has only 3 teeth. His brother Itty Bitty Monster has 4 times as many teeth. How many teeth does Itty Bitty have?

2. Mean Monster learned 6 letters in kindergarten. He learned 3 times as many in first grade. How many did he learn in first grade?

3. Mean Monster ate 5 sandwiches for lunch on Thursday. He ate 4 times as many sandwiches on Friday. How many sandwiches did he eat on Friday?

4. Mean Monster ate 5 **P's**. He ate 6 times as many **B's**. How many **B's** did he eat?

5. In the first play of the game, Mean Monster gained 7 yards. On the next play, he gained 4 times as many yards. How many yards did he gain on the second play?

6. Itty Bitty Monster broke 2 fingers trying to catch a coconut. Mean Monster broke 5 times as many fingers trying to catch a brick. How many fingers did Mean Monster break?

Wacky Waldo's Snow Show

Name _____

Wacky Waldo's Snow Show is an exciting and fantastic sight. Waldo has trained whales and bears to skate together on the ice. There is a hockey game between a team of sharks and a pack of wolves. Elephants ride sleds down steep hills. Horses and buffaloes ski swiftly down mountains.

1. Wacky Waldo has 4 ice-skating whales. He has 4 times as many bears who ice skate. How many bears can ice skate?

2. **Waldo's Snow Show** has 4 shows on Thursday, but it has 6 times as many shows on Saturday. How many shows are there on Saturday?

3. The Sharks' hockey team has 3 white sharks. It has 6 times as many tiger sharks. How many tiger sharks does it have?

4. The Wolves' hockey team has 4 gray wolves. It has 8 times as many red wolves. How many red wolves does it have?

5. Waldo taught 6 buffaloes to ski. He was able to teach 5 times as many horses to ski. How many horses did he teach?

6. Buff, a skiing buffalo, took 7 nasty spills when he was learning to ski. His friend Harry Horse fell down 8 times as often. How many times did Harry fall?

Bob Z. Cat

Name _____

Bob Z. Cat is a very strange cat. He is terrified of mice, and his best friends are dogs. He loves to read when he takes a bubble bath.

1. Bob Z. Cat ran away from 3 mice on Saturday. On Sunday, he ran away from 6 times as many mice. How many did he run from on Sunday?

2. Bob eats 7 cans of tuna fish in a week. How many cans would he eat in 5 weeks?

3. Bob Cat loves to read books. Last week, he read 4 books. This week, he has read 9 times as many. How many has he read this week?

4. Bob read 4 mystery stories one day and 7 times as many the next day. How many mysteries did he read the second day?

5. Bob Z. Cat spent only 9 minutes in his bath yesterday. Today, he spent 9 times as long relaxing in his bubble bath. How long did he bathe today?

6. Bob Z. Cat can purr 9 times a minute. How many times can he purr in 8 minutes?

Lizzy the Lizard— Brave Explorer

Name _____

1. Lizzy the Lizard went exploring through the woods. She saw 60 red ants. She saw 5 times as many black ants. How many black ants did she see?

2. Lizzy counted 40 snails in a field. She counted 7 times as many in a garden. How many were in the garden?

3. Lizzy found a tree full of termites. She ate only 30 termites, but she counted 7 times as many of them. How many termites did she count?

4. Lizzy counted 90 bees in a flower bed. She was chased by 6 times as many bees when she accidentally found their hive. How many bees chased her?

5. Lizzy counted 40 porcupine quills in an hour. She counted 6 times as many quills in a day. How many quills did she count in a day?

6. Lizzy counted 50 caterpillars on an apple tree and 7 times as many on a peach tree. How many were on the peach tree?

7. Lizzy discovered a nest of crickets. She ate 20 of them and left 8 times as many. How many did she leave?

Shifty Sam's Shop

Name _____

Shifty Sam's store is a messy jumble of things. Anything a child could want is there if it can be found under the piles of junk and stuff. But be careful if you buy anything. Check Sam's multiplication!

1. Mighty Man comics cost 13¢ at Shifty Sam's. You buy 4 of these comics. How much should you pay?

2. Your sister decides to buy 2 copies of the latest hit record by the Bird Brains. Each copy costs 89¢. How much will she pay?

3. Your best friend bought 9 marbles at Shifty's. Each marble cost 19¢. How much money did he spend?

4. Crazy stickers cost 21¢ each at Sam's. You buy 7 of them. How much should you pay?

5. Baseball cards are 11¢ each at Shifty Sam's. How much will it cost you for 8 cards?

6. Stinky Stickers have a skunk odor. Your best friend bought 7 Stinky Stickers which cost 18¢ each. How much did he spend?

Molly Mugwumps

Name _____

Molly Mugwumps is the toughest kid in school. She picks fights with kindergarteners and spends more time in the office than the principal does.

1. Molly is the toughest football player in her school. She ran for 23 yards on one play and went 3 times as far on the next play. How far did she run the second time?

2. Molly keeps a rock collection. She has 31 rocks in one sack. She has 7 times as many under her bed. How many rocks are under her bed?

3. Molly had 42 marbles when she came to school. She went home with 4 times as many. How many did she go home with?

4. Molly stuffed 21 sticks of gum in her mouth in the morning. In the afternoon, she crammed 9 times as many sticks into her mouth. How many sticks did she have in the afternoon?

5. Molly got 51 problems wrong in math last week. This week, she missed 8 times as many. How many did she miss this week?

6. Molly was sent to the office 21 days last year. This year, she was sent 7 times as often. How many days did she go this year?

IF8746 Math Topics

Bargain Bonanza at Pat's Pet Place

Name _____

Pat is having a gigantic sale at his place. Help him divide his animals into groups for the sale.

1. Pat got 84 rabbits. He is putting 4 rabbits in each cage. How many cages does he need?

2. Pat sells guppies in plastic bags with 5 guppies in each bag. He has 195 guppies. How many plastic bags does he need?

3. Pat has 392 white mice. They are kept in cages of 7 mice each. How many cages does Pat need?

4. Pat has 324 goldfish. If he puts 6 goldfish in each bag, how many plastic bags will he need?

5. Pat received 116 hamsters. He keeps them in cages of 4 each. How many cages does he need for his hamsters?

6. Pat has 120 parrots. They live in bird cages with 3 to each cage. How many bird cages does Pat need?

Wacky Waldo's Insect Business

Name _____

Wacky Waldo, world famous animal trainer, has trained insects to do all kinds of work. He has taught ants to carry bricks and grasshoppers to sing "Yankee Doodle." Cockroaches have been taught to cut hair, and flies have been taught to paint houses.

1. A cockroach can give 9 haircuts in a day. How many haircuts can 31 cockroaches give?

2. An ant can put 8 bricks on a wall in a day. How many bricks can 56 ants put on a wall in that time?

3. A chorus of grasshoppers sings "Yankee Doodle" 44 times in a day. How many times do they sing in 9 days?

4. It takes 76 flies to paint a wall. How many flies does it take to paint 4 walls?

5. A hard-working termite can saw 65 boards in a day. How many boards can 7 termites saw?

6. Waldo has taught lice to give shampoos. A louse can give 7 shampoos in a day. How many shampoos can it give in 25 days?

Sam Sillicook's Doughnut Shoppe

Name _____

Sam Sillicook believes that you should put a little jelly in your belly. He has invented the Super Duper Jelly Doughnuts that are so full of jelly, they leak. His Twisted Circles are drenched in sugar. He has also invented the Banana Cream Doughnut and Jam-jammed Cream Puffs.

1. Your teacher bought 32 Jam-jammed Cream Puffs. They cost $.89 each. How much did your teacher spend?

2. Harry D. Hulk bought 14 Banana Cream Doughnuts for his breakfast at $.65 each. How much did they cost Harry?

3. Your best friend bought 12 Twisted Circles at $.29 each. How much did he spend?

4. You love Jam-jammed Cream Puffs. Your mother buys 17 for your birthday party at $.89 each. How much do they cost?

5. Your principal decided to treat the teachers. He bought 24 Super Duper Jelly Doughnuts at $.49 each. What was the total cost?

6. Your class was treated to 40 Banana Cream Doughnuts which cost $.65 each. What was the total?

Buggs I. Lyke

Name _____

Buggs I. Lyke is in the fast food business. He is the famous inventor of the Beetle Burger which he sells at his store called **Beetle in a Box.**

1. It takes 300 beetles to make 6 Beetle Burgers. How many beetles are in each Beetle Burger?

2. Buggs I. Lyke sold 32 orders of Fried Flies on Monday. He sold 6 times as many orders on Saturday. How many orders of Fried Flies were sold on Saturday?

3. In July, 342 Cocoon Colas were sold. In August, 298 Cocoon Colas were sold. How many Colas were sold altogether?

4. There are 35 flies in a regular order of Fried Flies. There are 52 flies in a large order. How many more flies are in a large order?

5. Buggs uses 69 cocoons to make 3 Cocoon Colas. How many cocoons does it take for one cola?

6. Buggs sold 145 Beetle Burgers on the first day of school. On the next day, he sold 132 Beetle Burgers. How many did he sell in all?

Animal Trivia

Name _____

1. A wood rat has a tail which is 23.6 cm long. A deer mouse has a tail 12.2 cm long. What is the difference?

2. A rock mouse is 26.1 cm long. His tail adds another 14.4 cm. What is his total length from his nose to the tip of his tail?

3. A spotted bat has a tail 4.9 cm long. An evening bat has a tail 3.7 cm long. What is the difference?

4. A pocket gopher has a hind foot 3.5 cm long. A ground squirrel's hind foot is 6.4 cm long. How much longer is the ground squirrel's foot?

5. A cottontail rabbit has ears which are 6.8 cm long. A jackrabbit has ears 12.9 cm long. How much shorter is the cottontail's ear?

6. A porcupine has a tail 30.0 cm long. A possum has a tail 53.5 cm long. How much longer is the possum's tail?

7. The hind foot of a river otter is 14.6 cm long. The hind foot of a hog-nosed skunk is 9.0 cm long. What is the difference?

 IF8746 Math Topics

The Mystery of the Missing Sweets

Name _____

Some mysterious person is sneaking away with pieces of desserts from Sam Sillicook's Diner. Help him figure out how much is missing.

1. What fraction of Sam's Super Sweet Chocolate Cream Cake is missing?

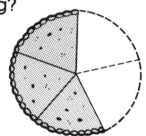

2. What fraction of Sam's Heavenly Tasting Cherry Cream Tart is missing?

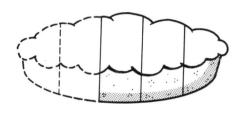

3. What fraction of Sam's Tastee Toffee Coffee Cake is missing?

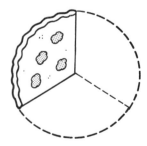

4. What fraction of Sam's Luscious Licorice Candy Cake is missing?

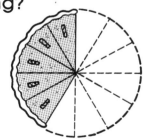

5. What fraction of Sam's Tasty Tidbits of Chocolate Ice Cream is missing?

6. Sam's Upside-down Ice Cream Cake is very famous. What fraction has vanished?

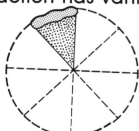

IF8746 Math Topics

Nat Nit Wit

Name _____

Nat Nit Wit can't tell time. He thinks that a minute is some kind of insect and that a clock is a new kind of soccer ball. He needs your help to solve these problems.

1. Nat is supposed to be at school in 10 minutes. What time should he get there?

_____

2. Nat started breakfast at 7:10 a.m. It took him 15 minutes to eat. Mark the time he finished.

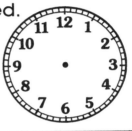

3. Nat will leave school in 5 minutes. What time will it be then?

_____

4. Nat and his brother Not Nit Wit will eat dinner in 15 minutes. When will that be?

_____

5. It is now 6:45 p.m. Nat must start his homework in 5 minutes. Mark the starting time on the clock.

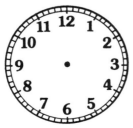

6. Nat will go to the park in 15 minutes. It is now 1:25 p.m. Mark the time he will go to the park.

Lizzy the Lizard Bags Her Bugs

Name _____

Lizzy the Lizard is a great hunter of insects. She separates her bugs into separate bags so that her lunch is ready for the week. Help her decide how to divide the bugs.

1. Lizzy bagged 45 cockroaches. She put 5 into each bag. How many bags did she use?

2. Lizzy found 32 termites. She put 4 into each bag. How many bags did she need?

3. Lizzy captured 49 stinkbugs. She put them into 7 bags. How many stinkbugs were in each bag?

4. Lizzy captured 27 horn beetles. She used 3 bags. How many beetles went into each bag?

5. Lizzy lassoed 36 butterflies. She put 9 into each bag. How many bags did she need?

6. Lizzy went fishing and caught 48 water beetles. She used 6 bags for her catch. How many beetles went into each bag?

"Where's the Bugs?"

Name _____

Beetle in a Box wants your business. It claims that it uses more bugs in its Beetleburgers, Fried Flies and Cocoon Colas than its competition, **McMealworm's.** You be the judge by solving these problems.

BUGS PER BURGER

McMealworms   BUGS IN A BOX

1. The chef at **Beetle in a Box** used 180 beetles to make 6 Beetleburgers. How many beetles were used in each burger?

2. The chef at **McMealworm's** used 203 mealworms to make 7 McMealworm Burgers. How many mealworms were used in each burger?

3. The fry cook at **Beetle in a Box** used 207 flies to make 9 orders of Fried Flies. How many flies were in each order?

4. The fry cook at **McMealworm's** used 176 cockroaches to make 8 orders of Roasted Roaches. How many roaches were in each order?

5. It took 140 cocoons to make 7 Cocoon Colas. How many cocoons were used in each Cola?

6. It took 114 crickets to make 6 Cricket Colas. How many crickets were in each Cola?

Buggs I. Lyke

Name _____

Buggs I. Lyke is the world famous owner of such fast food restaurants as **Beetle in a Box** and **McMealworm's.** He uses piles of insects in his restaurants. Help him arrange his insects.

1. Buggs uses 30 beetles in his Beetleburger. He has 750 beetles. How many Beetleburgers can he make?

2. Buggs uses 20 mealworms in his Mealburger. How many Mealburgers can he make from 740 mealworms?

3. A Cocoon Cola needs 20 cocoons to get the right flavor. How many Cocoon Colas can he make from 2,440 cocoons?

4. Buggs needs 30 mealworms for his Jumbo Mealburger. How many Jumbo Mealburgers can he make from 960 mealworms?

5. A large order of Fried Flies uses 60 flies. How many orders of Fried Flies can Buggs make from 3,120 flies?

6. Buggs makes Moth Shakes. Each shake uses 50 moths. How many shakes can he get from 850 moths?

Pat's Pets Aplenty

Name _____

Pat has just received an enormous shipment of animals to stock his new store, **Pat's Pets Aplenty.** He needs help separating his animals so that the cats don't end up in the fish tanks and the goldfish don't have to try swimming in the dog cages.

1. Pat received 650 rabbits. He wants to put them in pens of 25 rabbits each. How many rabbit pens does he need?

2. His shipment came with 828 white mice. Pat keeps them in cages of 23 each. How many cages does he need?

3. Pat was sent 1,620 guppies. If he puts 54 guppies in a plastic bag, how many plastic bags will he need?

4. The delivery truck dropped off 465 puppies. Each puppy pen holds 15 puppies. How many puppy pens does Pat need?

5. Pat was sent 253 king snakes. Each snake tank holds 11 snakes. How many snake tanks does Pat need?

6. Pat received 546 parrots. He keeps them in bird cages with 13 birds in each cage. How many bird cages does Pat need?

Smelly Belly Makes Sense, Cents and Scents

Name _____

Smelly Belly is a skunk with a great fondness for making perfumes. She also likes to make money. She considers this a very sensible thing to do.

Eau de Skunk $7.99

---

1. Smelly Belly's favorite perfume is called Eau de Skunk or Skunk Water. A bottle sells for $7.99. How much will it cost for 3 bottles?

2. Hefty Pig bought a bottle of Eau de Skunk for $7.99 and a bottle of Sweet Stink for $3.78. How much did it cost for both perfumes?

---

3. Smelly sold a bottle of her cheapest perfume, Polecat, to a rat for $1.99. How much less expensive is Polecat than Sweet Stink?

4. Smelly split 140 bottles of Skunk Musk evenly between her 7 sisters. How many bottles did each sister get?

---

5. Smelly sold 30 bottles of her Eau de Skunk at $7.99 each. How much money did she get?

6. A bottle of Skunk Cologne for Men costs $7.00 for 7 ounces. How much does each ounce cost?

Percy C. Porcupine: Student for a Day

Name _____

Percy C. Porcupine loves to learn, so one day he decided to follow his friends to school. He ended up in the 4th grade.

4th Grade

1. Percy spent 55 minutes in math, 65 minutes in reading and 25 minutes in spelling. What was the total time he spent in the classes?

2. Percy loves books. He ate 22 pages from his math book and 10 times as many from his reading book. How many pages did he eat from his reading book?

3. All 30 children in Percy's class wanted some quills. He split 180 quills evenly among them. How many quills did each child get?

4. Kathy and Ellen decided to pet Percy. Kathy got 131 quills in her hand, and Ellen got 97 quills in her hand. What was the difference?

5. Percy read 15 words in a minute. At this rate, how many words did he read in 25 minutes?

6. At morning recess, Percy played tag, and he tagged 16 children. He gave each one 27 quills. How many quills did Percy give out?

Molly Mugwumps

Name _____

Molly Mugwumps is the best football player but not the best student in the 4th grade. She thinks math and marbles are both something to eat.

1. Molly got a 60%, a 40% and a 20% on 3 spelling tests. What was her average mark? (HINT: Add the scores and divide by 3.)

2. Molly rushed for 60 yards in one game, 80 yards in a second game and 70 yards in a third. What was her average number of yards rushing?

3. Molly took 5 math tests. She got a 35%, a 45%, a 25%, a 50% and a 0%. What was her average mark?

4. Molly missed the following number of problems on her math papers: 12, 20, 4, 7 and 2. What was her average number of wrong answers?

5. Molly drank 12 quarts of milk one week, 20 quarts the second week and 28 quarts the third week. What was her weekly average?

6. Molly doesn't do very well on tests. She got a 28%, a 34%, a 22% and a 12% on her last 4 social studies tests. What was her average grade?

Shifty Sam's "Super Duper Sale"

Name _____

Shifty Sam owns a store where you can buy just about anything from sports equipment to the latest fads in clothes and records. But you have to be very careful, or Shifty Sam will cheat you.

1. Shifty Sam sells posters at $.99 each or 3 posters for $2.99 during his sale. Is this a good deal? How much more or less is this than the regular price?

2. You can buy Spiffle balls that curve and loop for $.67 regularly. Shifty has them on sale now at 5 for $2.99. Do you save money buying them this way? How much?

3. Sam's Potato Patch Dolls usually sell for $3.99 each. During his sale, they are 2 for $8.99. How much more or less is this than the regular price?

4. The normal price for a package of stickers is $.49. The sale price is 5 for $2.49. Is this a good deal? What is the difference in the cost?

5. A package of Juicy Spurts Bubble Gum costs $.39. During the sale, Sam is selling 7 packs for $2.39. How much do you save at the sale price?

6. Sam will sell Iron-On Tee Shirt Designs at $.89 each or 4 for $3.49 during his Super Duper Sale. How much money is saved this way?

Birthday Party at McMealworm's

Name _____

Your mother decides to let you invite your friends to a birthday party at your favorite restaurant, **McMealworm's.** A McMealworm Burger costs $1.69. A large order of Roasted Roaches costs $.79. A Cricket Cola is $.89.

1. For an appetizer, your mother buys 7 large orders of Roasted Roaches. How much change will she get from a $10.00 bill?

2. Your friends drink 11 Cricket Colas before dinner. How much will these cost? How much less than $10.00 is this?

3. One of your best friends orders 2 McMealworm Burgers and 3 Cricket Colas. What does it cost for his meal?

4. Another friend pigs out and buys 6 large orders of Roasted Roaches and 1 McMealworm Burger. What does it cost for that meal?

5. One of the girls orders 2 McMealworm Burgers and 2 Cricket Colas. What does it cost for her meal?

6. The total cost of the party to your mom is exactly $90.00. What is the average cost for your group of 7 boys, 7 girls and 1 parent? (HINT: Find the total number of people and divide.)

Suzy Spider — Interior Decorator

Name _____

Suzy Spider is decorating her house. She is a very clever decorator, but she needs your help figuring out the area and perimeter.

Key Facts:
- Perimeter is the sum of all four sides.
- Area is the length times the width.

1. Suzy is putting a silk fence around her garden. It is 12 cm long and 10 cm wide. What is the perimeter of the garden?

2. Suzy Spider wants to surround her house with a silk thread. Her house is 17 cm long and 12 cm wide. What is its perimeter?

3. Suzy wants to carpet her living room. It is 5 cm long and 4 cm wide. How much carpet should she buy for her living room?

4. Suzy wants to put wallpaper on a kitchen wall. The wall is 7 cm tall and 4 cm wide. What is its area?

5. Suzy has decided to hang a silk thread all the way around her porch. The porch is 4 cm long and 3 cm wide. How long should the thread be?

6. Suzy's bedroom is 6 cm long and 5 cm wide. How much carpet should she buy for it?

Krab E. Krabby

Name _____

Krab E. Krabby carries a yardstick with him everywhere he goes, and he measures everything that he can.

Key Facts:
   12 inches = 1 foot
   36 inches = 3 feet = 1 yard

---

1. Krab E. Krabby wanted to measure the length of a grasshopper. Would he use a ruler or a yardstick?

2. Krab E. Krabby scolded Rollo Rattlesnake because Rollo wouldn't straighten out and cooperate. Should Krab E. Krabby use a ruler or a yardstick to measure Rollo?

3. Mr. Krabby measured a garter snake that was 44 inches long. How many yards and inches was this?
_____ yard _____ inches left over

4. Krab E. measured a tomato hornworm that was 5 inches long. How many inches less than a foot was this?

5. Mr. Krabby measured a monarch butterfly that was 4 inches wide. How many inches less than a foot was the butterfly?

6. Krab E. Krabby measured a lazy tuna that was 1 foot 11 inches long. How many total inches was the tuna?

Knowing When to Add – I

Learn these key addition words. They will help you know when to add.

 more
total in all
in addition to  altogether
sum

Circle the key addition words
and solve the problems.

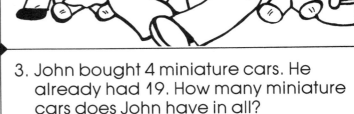

1. George has 6 railroad cars. Chuck
has 8 railroad cars. If they join their
railroad cars, how many cars
altogether will be in their train?

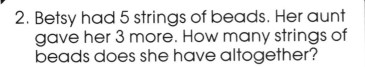

$6 \oplus 8 = $ _____

2. Betsy had 5 strings of beads. Her aunt
gave her 3 more. How many strings of
beads does she have altogether?

3. John bought 4 miniature cars. He
already had 19. How many miniature
cars does John have in all?

4. Emily has 15 dolls in her collection at
home. When the 13 dolls which are in
the doll hospital are returned, how
many will she have in all?

5. Molly already had 96 pictures in her
album. Then she added 17 more. How
many pictures in all does she now
have in her album?

6. Dean collected 439 baseball cards.
Uncle Ben gave him 72 more. How
many baseball cards does Dean
have altogether?

7. Jim had 84 seashells in his collection.
He found 25 more. Altogether, how
many seashells does he have?

Name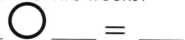

Knowing When to Add – II

Circle the key addition words and solve the problems.

1. Jane and her parents rented a lake cottage for two weeks. The first week's rent was $120.00. The second week's rent was $90.00. How much in all was the rent for two weeks?

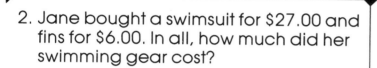

2. Jane bought a swimsuit for $27.00 and fins for $6.00. In all, how much did her swimming gear cost?

3. The rent on a boat is $8.00 per day, and the rent for a motor is $7.00 per day. How much altogether would it cost to rent the boat and motor for a day?

4. It is a 3-mile walk from the cottage to a road on the other side of the lake. It is a 4-mile walk down the road to get to town. How far is it altogether to walk from the cottage to town?

5. On the first day she was at the lake, Jane caught 7 fish. Her parents caught 12 more fish than she did. How many fish did Jane's parents catch?

6. Jane bought 65¢ worth of bait in addition to the 30¢ worth she already had. How much bait did Jane have altogether?

7. During the first week Jane spent 28 hours out on the lake. During the second week she was on the lake only 13 hours. How many hours in all did Jane spend on the lake?

Knowing When to Add – Review

Circle the key addition words and solve the problems.

1. The choir at Madison School is made up of 26 girls and 18 boys. What is the total choir membership?

____ ◯ ____ = ____

2. The band at Madison School is composed of 19 girls and 22 boys. How many band members are there in all?

3. There are 214 girls and 263 boys attending Madison School. How many students altogether attend Madison School?

4. Next fall, in addition to the 477 students already at Madison, 248 more will be bussed in. Altogether, how many students will be at Madison School?

5. Mr. Mill's bus route is 14 miles long. Mrs. Albert's route is 17 miles long. Ms. Byrne's route is 15 miles long. How many miles altogether do these 3 bus routes cover?

6. The book rental at Madison is $8.00. The supplies cost $14.00. The locker fee is $3.00. What is the sum of these expenses?

7. The staff at Madison is made up of 24 teachers, 3 custodians and 2 administrators. How many staff members in all are there?

Knowing When to Subtract – I

Circle the key subtraction words and solve the problems.

Learn these key subtraction words.
They will help you know when to subtract.

> fewer
> less
> left
> more

1. Bill and his father planted corn on 120 acres of the farm. They planted wheat on 80 acres. How many fewer acres of wheat did they plant than corn?

120 ⊖ 80 = ___

2. Bill's father sold 16 of his 34 beef cattle. How many cattle were left?

3. Bill picked 34 quarts of strawberries. Bill's mother froze 13 of those quarts. How many quarts were left for Bill to sell?

4. For his Four-H Club project, Bill is raising 12 hogs. His father has 40 hogs. How many fewer hogs does Bill have than his father?

5. Last week Bill's father picked 78 bushels of apples. Bill picked 14 bushels. How many more bushels did his father pick than Bill?

6. Bill and his father picked 128 ears of corn and sold 72 of the ears of corn from their roadside stand. How many ears of corn were left?

Name _____

Knowing When to Subtract – II

Circle the key subtraction words and solve the problems.

1. Jenny and Bob ate lunch at the local burger shop. Jenny paid $1.49 for a cheeseburger. Bob paid $1.25 for a hamburger. How much less did Bob's sandwich cost than Jenny's?

2. Jenny had $5.00. She spent $2.49 on her lunch. How much money does she have left?

3. Chili dogs are 99¢ each and hot dogs are 79¢ each. How much less is a hot dog than a chili dog?

4. The manager said that yesterday he sold 249 hamburgers and 123 hot dogs. How many more hamburgers were sold than hot dogs?

5. Jenny ate a soft ice cream cone which cost 45¢ less than Bob's 95¢ chocolate sundae. How much did the ice cream cone cost?

6. This afternoon 27 adults and 15 children were eating in the burger shop. How many more adults were there than children?

7. Bill's lunch cost $2.15. Bob's lunch cost $2.60. How much less did Bill pay for his lunch than Bob?

Name _____

Knowing When to Subtract – Review

Circle the key subtraction words and solve the problems.

1. There are 71 restaurants and 58 grocery stores in Lexington. How many fewer grocery stores than restaurants are there?

2. In one part of Lexington 28 of the 113 houses were torn down. How many houses were left standing?

3. Lexington has 53 elementary schools and 18 middle schools. How many more elementary schools than middle schools does Lexington have?

4. There are 980 doctors and 314 auto mechanics in Lexington. How many more doctors are there than mechanics?

5. There are 17 fewer theaters than churches in Lexington. Lexington has 41 churches. How many theaters are there?

6. Lexington has 364 miles of two-lane streets and 178 miles of four-lane streets. How many more miles of two-lane streets than four-lane streets does Lexington have?

7. Lexington has 12 fewer traffic lights than Knoxville does. Knoxville has 237 traffic lights. How many traffic lights does Lexington have?

Name _____

Add or Subtract? – Review

Circle the key addition and subtraction words. Then solve the problems.

1. The bakery donated 84 doughnuts for the sunrise breakfast. Of the 84 doughnuts, 65 were eaten. How many doughnuts were left uneaten?

2. The baker baked 204 cookies. He added chocolate chips to 96 of them. How many cookies were left without chocolate chips?

3. Tom ate 12 cookies. Bill ate 13 cookies. Ann ate 11 cookies. What was the total number of cookies eaten?

4. The baker baked 37 apple pies and 44 pumpkin pies. How many more pumpkin pies than apple pies did he bake?

5. The baker iced 172 doughnuts and dipped 137 fewer doughnuts in powdered sugar. How many doughnuts were dipped in powdered sugar?

6. In one week the baker sold 192 layer cakes, in addition to 265 sheet cakes. How many cakes did he sell altogether?

7. Yesterday the baker sold 72 peach pies, 49 banana cream pies and 12 sugar cream pies. That is a total of how many pies?

Name _____

Knowing When to Multiply — I

Learn these key words. They will help you know when to multiply.

times   each   per   in all   altogether

Circle the key multiplication words and solve the problems.

1. There are 6 baseball teams in the city league. Each team has 9 players. How many players in all are there in the city league?

6 9 = _____

2. The baseball team made an average of 3 errors per game. The team played 12 games. How many errors were made altogether?

3. The basketball team averaged 62 points per game. The team played 20 games this season. How many points did the team score in all?

4. A baseball glove costs $38.00. How much altogether would it cost to buy 9 gloves?

5. Each player's uniform costs $53.00. In all, how much would it cost to outfit 9 players?

6. Jeff swam 35 laps in the pool each day for 30 days. How many laps did he swim altogether?

7. Swim trunks cost $4.00 each. It costs 65 times that much to outfit a football player. How much would it cost to outfit a football player?

<u>Name</u>

Knowing When to Multiply — II

Circle the key multiplication words and solve the problems.

Learn these key words. They will help you know when to multiply.

per
times
each
altogether
in all

1. Emily works in her father's fruit and vegetable stand on weekends. She worked 8 hours each Saturday for 4 weeks. How many hours altogether did Emily work during those 4 weeks?

2. Apples sell for 30¢ each. How much would 3 apples cost?

3. Emily found that each orange weighs 8 ounces. How much in all would 12 oranges weigh?

4. A large bag of grapefruit sells for 2 times the price of a bag of onions. The bag of onions sells for $1.30. What is the price of the large bag of grapefruit?

5. Mr. Long bought a bunch of bananas which weighed 3 pounds. Bananas sell for 32¢ per pound. How much in all did the bananas cost?

6. Grocery bags cost 3¢ each. During one morning Emily used 27 different bags. Altogether, how much did the bags cost?

<u>Name</u>

Knowing When to Multiply — III

Circle the key multiplication words and solve the problems.

---

1. Jack cuts and sells firewood. He cuts 6 cords of firewood per day. How many cords does he cut in 5 days?

2. Firewood sells for $32.00 per cord. How much money does Jack receive in all for 6 cords?

---

3. Jack sold $128.00 worth of firewood to one customer and 7 times that amount to a store owner. How much did the store owner pay Jack?

4. If Jack cuts and sells 30 cords of wood, how much would Jack receive altogether at $32.00 per cord?

5. Chain saw blades sell for $6.50 each. Jack buys 5 each week. How much in all does Jack spend for chain saw blades during one week?

---

6. Each day Jack uses 4 gallons of gasoline in his chain saw. How many gallons altogether does Jack use in 5 days?

7. Gasoline costs Jack $3.68 per day. In all, what is his cost for gasoline for 5 days?

<u>Name</u>

Multiply or Add?

Circle the key multiplication and addition words and solve the problems.

1. The Davis family went on a 7-day trip. They averaged 420 miles per day. How many miles in all did they travel?

2. The Davis family usually drove 55 miles per hour. How many miles in all could they cover in 6 hours at this speed?

3. On the second day of the trip, Mr. Davis ran over some glass and had to replace 2 tires. The cost was $80.00 per tire. Altogether, how much did the tire replacement cost?

4. On the second day they traveled only 170 miles. On the third they covered 540 miles. How many miles altogether did they travel during those days?

5. The Davis family ate in 3 different restaurants on each of the 7 days. Altogether, in how many different restaurants did they eat?

6. During the first 3 days of the trip, the Davis family traveled through 34 towns. During the last 4 days they went through 37 towns. How many towns did they travel through in all?

7. On the last day of the trip, the Davis family left for home at 6:00 A.M. and arrived 9 hours later. They drove at the average rate of 50 miles per hour. How far did they travel in all on the last day?

Multiply or Subtract?

Circle the key multiplication and subtraction words and solve the problems.

1. Bill works 3 hours per day in a tire store. How many hours altogether does Bill work in 5 days?

2. There are 94 auto tires and 37 truck tires in the store. How many fewer truck tires are there than auto tires?

3. The store had 94 auto tires in stock. One day Bill sold 16 auto tires. How many of the 94 auto tires were left?

4. The manager told Bill to order 3 times as many auto tires as truck tires. Bill ordered 18 truck tires. How many auto tires should he order?

5. Each truck tire weighs 80 pounds. How much altogether do 6 truck tires weigh?

6. A truck tire weighs 80 pounds. An auto tire weighs 18 pounds. How many more pounds does a truck tire weigh than an auto tire?

7. The 4 tires for a Ford car cost $184.00. The 4 tires for a Dodge car cost $240.00. How much less do the tires cost for the Ford than the Dodge?

<u>Name</u>

Knowing When to Divide – I

Learn these key words. They will help you know when to divide.

each   per

Circle the key division words and solve the problems.

1. While at the grocery store with her mother, Doris spent 36¢ for pencils. The pencils cost 6¢ each. How many pencils did she buy?

   36¢ ÷ 6¢ = _____

2. Doris's mother bought 2 bags of apples for $2.40. How much did she pay per bag?

3. The 2 bags of apples together contained 16 apples. How many apples were in each bag?

4. The grocer sold 3 oranges for 39¢. That is how much per orange?

5. Doris bought 4 rolls of mints for 96¢. How much did she pay for each roll?

6. Doris bought a package of 30 cookies. If the cookies were divided evenly between the 5 members of Doris's family, how many cookies would each person get?

7. Doris's mother bought 4 pounds of meat which cost her $8.80. What was the price per pound?

<u>Name</u>

Knowing When to Divide — II

Circle the key division words and solve the problems.

Learn these key words. They will help you know when to divide.

each   per

1. The track team had 28 athletes trying out for 4 open positions. That is an average of how many athletes per position?

2. The girls' and the boys' basketball teams have the same record of wins. Together they won 28 games. That is how many wins per team?

3. In a recent game 6 basketball players scored 42 points. How many points is that per player?

4. The baseball team played 8 games away from home. The team traveled 96 miles. That is an average of how many miles per trip?

5. 92 practice suits were issued to those students trying out for 4 different athletic teams. If the same number of suits were issued for each sport, how many students were out for each sport?

6. During 5 days of practice the basketball team used 75 towels. How many towels were used per day?

Name _____

Knowing When to Divide — III

Circle the key division words and solve the problems.

1. The 7 members of Dan's scout troop earned $56.00 for new equipment. How much per scout was earned?

2. On the scouts' camping trip Dan took 24 pictures. How many rolls of film did Dan use if each roll takes 8 pictures?

3. On the camping trip the 7 scouts ate 42 hot dogs. How many hot dogs per scout were eaten?

4. At breakfast 21 eggs were eaten by the 7 scouts. How many eggs were eaten per scout?

5. Later 5 of the scouts caught a total of 35 fish. How many fish did each scout catch?

6. The troop took a 4-hour hike and covered 16 miles. How many miles per hour did the troop cover?

7. During the morning exercises the 7 scouts did a total of 168 sit-ups. How many sit-ups per scout were done?

Knowing When to Divide — IV

Circle the key division words and solve the problems.

1. Susan worked 9 arithmetic problems in 54 minutes. How many minutes did she use for each problem?

2. Jeff worked 9 problems in 63 minutes. He used how many minutes per problem?

3. On an achievement test the class was allowed 27 minutes to work 9 problems. How many minutes were allowed for each problem?

4. On a recent test the teacher found that the class made 72 errors. That was an average of 3 errors per student. How many students are in the class?

5. The 5-member mathematics team won 35 ribbons this semester. How many ribbons per member were won?

6. The 5-member team winning the state math contest received $10,000 in scholarships. How much scholarship money did each member win?

7. The runner-up team in the state math contest received $7,500 in scholarships. How much scholarship money was awarded each of the 5 members?

Name _____

Add or Divide?

Circle the key addition and division words. Then solve the problems.

1. Pam read 32 books in 8 weeks. How many books did she read per week?

$$32 \div 8 = \underline{\hspace{2cm}}$$

2. Peter read 30 books in 6 weeks. How many books per week did Peter read?

3. The 14 girls in Pam's class read a total of 56 books. The 13 boys read a total of 39 books. How many books in all were read by Pam's classmates?

4. The library in Pam's school contains 96 books which Pam would like to read. If Pam reads 4 books each week, how many weeks will it take her to read them all?

5. Pam has 28 books in her own library. She was given 4 more books for her birthday. How many books in all does Pam now have?

6. Pam read 84 pages on Saturday, 51 pages on Sunday and 17 pages on Monday. How many pages in all did Pam read?

7. Pam bought 2 new books. One cost $4.50, and the other cost $3.50. How much altogether did Pam pay for the 2 books?

<u>Name</u>

Subtract or Divide?

Circle the key subtraction and division words. Then solve the problems.

1. The bus took 44 students to the Kennedy Space Center. Of the students, 19 were girls and 25 were boys. How many more boys were there than girls?

$$25 \ominus 19 = \underline{\hspace{2cm}}$$

2. While in space an astronaut has 34 different food choices. Jan has 7 food choices at home. How many fewer food choices does Jan have than an astronaut?

3. The equipment aboard the satellite will operate for 402 days. After one year (365 days) has passed, how many more days will the equipment work?

4. A 7-day week on Pluto would be 980 Earth hours long. How many hours are in each Pluto day?

5. A day on Mercury is 2,100 Earth hours long. A Venus day is 5,400 hours long. A day on Mercury is how many Earth hours fewer than a day on Venus?

6. Voyager came within 240,000 miles of Jupiter. That distance would be how many more miles than the 3,000 miles it takes to travel from New York to Seattle?

7. It takes the planet Uranus 84 years to revolve around the Sun. During that time Jupiter revolves around the Sun 7 times. How many years does each of Jupiter's revolutions take?

Multiply or Divide?

Circle the multiplication and division key words. Then solve the problems.

1. Tom is starting an orchard. He has 5 acres of land. Tom's father has an orchard that is 25 times as large as Tom's orchard. How many acres does his father's orchard cover?

2. Tom plans to plant 300 trees in his orchard over a period of 6 years. How many trees must he plant each year?

3. On one of his acres Tom has 11 times as many cherry trees as apple trees. He has 5 apple trees on that acre. How many cherry trees does he have?

4. Trees cost $7.00 each. How much altogether will 60 trees cost?

5. At $7.00 each, how much will the 300 trees in the orchard cost altogether?

6. It will cost Tom $240.00 to spray the trees in his 5-acre orchard. How much will it cost per acre to spray?

7. To get the orchard started, Tom borrowed $4,320.00. He will pay back the money over the next 6 years. How much will he pay each year?

<u>Name</u>

Review Problems

Circle the key words and solve the problems.

1. The 24 third grade students at Dogwood School, along with the 209 other Dogwood students, took part in the annual clean-up day. Altogether, how many students from Dogwood helped with the clean-up?

2. Students from 8 different rooms at Dogwood School collected a total of 128 bags of trash. How many bags per room is that?

3. The fourth grade students collected 4 bags fewer than the 17 bags the third grade students collected. How many bags of trash were collected by the fourth grade students?

4. While collecting trash, the Dogwood students also collected 28 pounds of aluminum cans. At 3¢ per pound, how much were the aluminum cans worth?

5. Dogwood students collected 128 bags of trash. This was 38 bags more than the Hickory Hills students collected. How many bags of trash did the Hickory Hills students collect?

6. Pickup trucks hauled the bags of trash away. One truck hauled 56 bags, and the other hauled 47 bags away. How many bags of trash were hauled altogether by the two trucks?

7. The newspaper published the winning essay "Keeping Our Community Clean." Of the 209 Dogwood students, 87 entered the contest. That left how many Dogwood students who did not enter the essay contest?

Name _____

Which Problem Is Correct? — I

One of the methods of solution at the left is correct for the problem. Pick the correct method of solution and finish solving the problem.

1.
```
    56        56
  + 17      − 17
  ____      ____
```
Bill and his friends collect baseball cards. Bill has 17 fewer cards than Mack. Bill has 56 cards. How many baseball cards does Mack have?

2.
```
    54        3 ⟌54
  x  3
  ____
```
Amos bought 54 baseball cards. He already had 3 times as many. How many baseball cards did Amos have before his latest purchase?

3.
```
   3.80       3.80
 + 3.50     − 3.50
 _____     _____
```
Joe paid $3.50 for a "Mickey Mantle" baseball card. "Ted Williams" cost him $3.80. How much more did he pay for "Ted Williams" than for "Mickey Mantle"?

4.
```
   3.60       9 ⟌3.60
 x    9
 _____
```
Will bought 9 baseball cards for $3.60. How much did he pay per card?

5.
```
   8.00       8.00
 +  .50     −  .50
 _____     _____
```
"Babe Ruth" baseball cards were selling for $8.00. "Herb Score" baseball cards sold for 50¢. "Herb Score" cards sold for how much less than "Babe Ruth" cards?

6.
```
   0.75       8 ⟌0.75
 x    8
 _____
```
Andy bought 8 baseball cards at 75¢ each. How much did Andy pay in all?

<u>Name</u>

Which Problem Is Correct? — II

The solution at the left is correct for one of the problems to the right. Draw a line under the problem that goes with the solution. Then compute the answer.

1.   6744
       −698

a) The local zoo has an elephant which weighs 6,744 pounds. The bear weighs 698 pounds. The bear weighs how much less than the elephant?

b) An elephant at the zoo weighs 6,744 pounds. The bear weighs 698 pounds. Together, how much do they weigh?

2.   12
      x 6

a) Each of the 6 lions at the zoo gets 12 pounds of meat to eat each day. How much meat is needed to feed the lions for one day?

b) 12 pounds of meat is shared each day by the 6 lions at the zoo. How much meat does each lion get?

3.   213
       +78

a) The zoo had 213 animals and gave 78 to another city that was starting a zoo. How many animals were left?

b) The zoo had 213 animals and was given 78 more. How many animals in all does the zoo have?

4.   4 ⌈36

a) The zoo has 4 times as many monkeys as zebras. There are 36 monkeys. How many zebras are there?

b) The zoo has 4 times as many zebras as monkeys. There are 36 monkeys. How many zebras are there?

5.   350
      x 7

a) Last week the attendance at the zoo was 350. How many people went to the zoo on each of the 7 days?

b) Last week the attendance at the zoo averaged 350 people per day. How many people went to the zoo during those 7 days?

6.   248
      x 2

a) Because of financial problems, the zoo must double attendance or double the ticket price. The average daily attendance is 248. What must attendance be so that the ticket price remains the same?

b) The average daily attendance at the zoo is 248. This is twice the number needed to meet costs. How many tickets must be sold to meet costs?

Which Problem Is Correct? — III

The solution at the left is correct for one of the problems to the right. Draw a line under the correct problem. Then compute the answer.

1. $\begin{array}{r} 16 \\ \times\ 8 \\ \hline \end{array}$

a) It is 8 times as far to Detroit as it is to Grandmother's house. It is 16 miles to Grandmother's house. How far is it to Detroit?

b) It is 8 times as far to Grandmother's house as to Detroit. It is 16 miles to Grandmother's house. How far is it to Detroit?

2. $2\overline{)1150}$

a) It is twice as far from Detroit to Des Moines as from Detroit to Dallas. It is 1,150 miles from Detroit to Dallas. How far is it from Detroit to Des Moines?

b) It is twice as far from Detroit to Dallas as it is from Detroit to Des Moines. It is 1,150 miles from Detroit to Dallas. How far is it from Detroit to Des Moines?

3. $\begin{array}{r} 8.15 \\ -6.75 \\ \hline \end{array}$

a) A bus ticket to Frankenmuth costs $8.15. A ticket to Detroit costs $6.75. How much do the 2 tickets cost altogether?

b) A bus ticket to Frankenmuth costs $8.15. A ticket to Detroit costs $6.75. How much more does it cost to go to Frankenmuth than to Detroit?

4. $\begin{array}{r} 150 \\ \times\ 8 \\ \hline \end{array}$

a) It is 150 miles round trip from Bob's home to the University of Michigan. In his freshman year Bob made the trip 8 times. How many miles altogether did he travel?

b) Bob made 8 trips to the University of Michigan. He traveled a total of 1,200 miles. How far did he travel on each trip?

5. $3\overline{)552}$

a) On vacation this year the Adams family traveled 552 miles. Last year they traveled 3 times as far. How many miles did they travel last year?

b) On vacation last year the Adams family traveled 3 times as far as they did this year. Last year they traveled 552 miles. How far did they travel this year?

6. $\begin{array}{r} 595 \\ \times\ 5 \\ \hline \end{array}$

a) The Willis family traveled across the U.S. in 5 days. They averaged 595 miles per day. How far did they travel in all?

b) The Willis family traveled 595 miles in 5 days. How far did they travel each day?

<u>Name</u>

Too Much Information — I

Each problem on this page contains a fact which is not needed in the solution. This unused fact is called a **distractor.** Underline the distractor in each problem. Then solve the problem.

1. Wild bird seed costs 23¢ per pound. The birds eat 81 pounds of wild bird seed each week. How many pounds of wild bird seed are needed for 52 weeks?

2. Wild bird seed costs 23¢ per pound. The birds eat 8 pounds of wild bird seed each week. How long will 200 pounds last?

3. One day 25 cardinals, 18 gold finches and 19 purple finches ate at the feeders. How many finches were fed?

4. One afternoon 26 titmice, 14 nuthatches and 17 downy woodpeckers visited the feeders. How many more titmice were there than nuthatches?

5. One morning 83 birds ate sunflower seeds, 27 birds ate wild bird seed and 19 birds ate earthworms. How many birds ate seed?

6. One morning 17 cardinals ate at the feeder containing sunflower seed. 14 robins and 12 towhees ate worms from the ground. Mr. Phillips figured each sunflower seed eater ate 3¢ worth. How much did the birds' sunflower seed feast cost Mr. Phillips?

7. Mr. Phillips spent $180.00 for sunflower seed and wild bird seed. The average cost was 30¢ per pound. He spent $34.50 on 150 pounds of wild bird seed. How much did he spend for 450 pounds of sunflower seed?

Too Much Information — II

Underline the **distractor** and solve the problems.

1. All 20 of the students from Sandy's class went to the movies. Tickets cost $1.50 each. Drinks cost 55¢ each. How much altogether did the students spend on tickets?

2. Of the students, 11 were girls and 9 were boys. At $1.50 per ticket, how much did the boys' tickets cost altogether?

3. While 5 students had ice cream, 12 others had candy. Ice cream cost 75¢ per cup. How much did the students spend on ice cream?

4. 7 of the 20 students did not like the movie. 3 of the 20 students had seen the movie before. How many students had not seen the movie before?

5. Mary paid 55¢ for an orange drink and 65¢ for a candy bar. Sarah paid 45¢ for popcorn. How much did Mary's refreshments cost her?

6. 6 of the students spent a total of $16.50 for refreshments and $9.00 for their tickets. How much did each spend for refreshments?

7. 10 of the students went back to see the movie again the next day. Each student paid $1.50 for a ticket, 45¢ for popcorn and 55¢ for a soft drink. How much did each student pay?

Name

Picture the Problem — I

Draw a picture of each problem. Then solve the problem.

1. Charley cut his pizza in 3rds and gave one piece to Sherry. George cut his pizza in 6ths and gave Sherry 3 pieces. Which boy gave Sherry the most pizza?

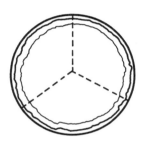 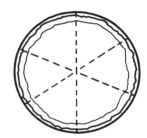

Charley   George

2. Harold cut a cherry pie into 6ths and a peach pie into 9ths. He ate 2 pieces of cherry pie and 2 pieces of peach pie. Which pie did he eat the most of?

Cherry   Peach

3. Sally cut her cake into 12ths. Sally ate 2 of the 12ths. Joe ate 1/4 of the cake. Who ate the most cake?

Joe   Sally

4. Betsy and Emily each bought a foot-long hot dog. Betsy divided her hot dog into 6 equal parts and gave Sam 1 of the 6ths. Emily divided her hot dog into 12 equal parts and gave Sam 2 of the 12ths. Who gave Sam the most hot dog?

 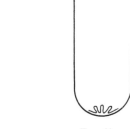

Betsy   Emily

<u>Name</u>

Picture the Problem — II

Draw a picture of each problem. Then solve the problem.

1. Andy had two ropes of the same length. He cut one rope into 2 equal parts and gave the 2 halves to Bill. The other rope he cut into 4ths and gave 2 of the 4ths to Sue. Who got the most rope?

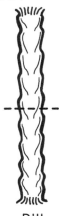 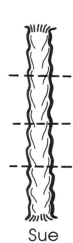

    Bill   Sue

2. Henry cut an 8-foot log into 4 equal pieces and burned 2 of them in the fireplace. Joseph cut an 8-foot log into 8 equal pieces and put 3 of them in the fireplace. Who put the most wood in the fireplace?

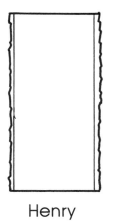 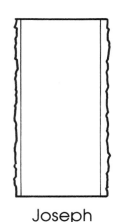

    Henry   Joseph

3. Mr. Johns built an office building with an aisle down the middle. He divided one side into 6 equal spaces. He divided the other side into 9 equal spaces. The Ace Company rented 5 of the 9ths. The Best Company rented 4 of the 6ths. Which company rented the larger space?

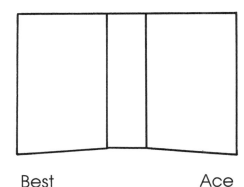

    Best   Ace

4. The 4-H Club display area at the state fair was divided into 2 equal areas. One of these sections had 12 booths, the other 9 booths. The flower display covered 3 of the 9ths, and the melon display covered 4 of the 12ths. Which display had the most room?

 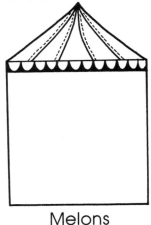

    Flowers   Melons

Name

Time Problems — I

Draw the hands on the clocks to show the starting time and the ending time.
Then write the answer to the problem.

1. Molly left school at 3:30 p.m. It took her 20 minutes to walk home. What time did she get home?

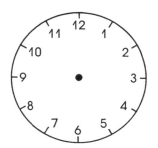

Answer:

2. John's ball game started at 4:05 p.m. and lasted for 2 hours and 30 minutes. What time did the game end?

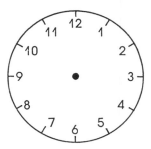

Answer:

3. Ann and Beth arrived at the ice cream store at 2:15 p.m. and left for home 40 minutes later. What time did they leave the ice cream store?

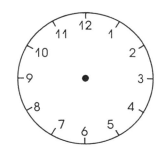

Answer:

4. The school day starts at 8:00 a.m. and ends 6 hours and 45 minutes later. What time does school end?

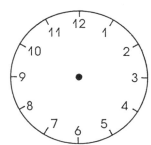

Answer:

5. Don's sister Beth was on the phone from 3:45 p.m. until 4:15 p.m. How long was Beth on the phone?

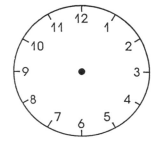

Answer:

6. Joyce started her bath at 8:35 p.m. and got out at 9:15 p.m. How long was Joyce in the bathtub?

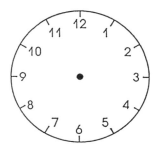

Answer:

Name _____

Time Problems — II

Draw the hands on the clocks to show the starting time and the ending time.
Then write the answer to the problem.

1. The bike race started at 2:55 p.m. and lasted 2 hours and 10 minutes. What time did the race end?

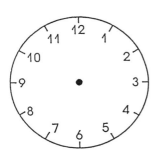 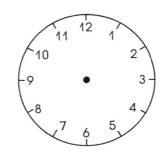

Answer: _____

2. Sherry walked in the 12-mile Hunger Walk. She started at 12:30 p.m. and finished at 4:50 p.m. How long did she walk?

 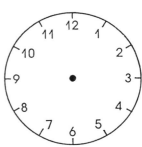

Answer: _____

3. The 500-mile auto race started at 11:00 a.m. and lasted 2 hours and 25 minutes. What time did the race end?

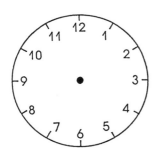 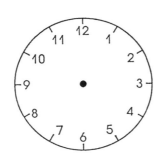

Answer: _____

4. The train left Indianapolis at 7:25 a.m. and arrived in Chicago at 10:50 a.m. How long did the trip take?

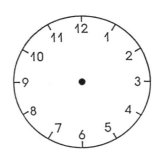 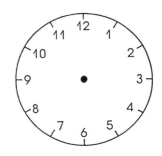

Answer: _____

5. The chili cook-off started at 10:00 a.m., and all the chili was cooked by 4:30 p.m. How long did it take to cook the chili?

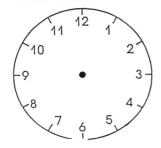 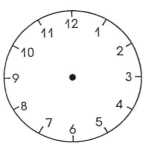

Answer: _____

6. The chili judging began at 4:30 p.m. After 3 hours and 45 minutes the chili had all been eaten. At what time was the chili judging finished?

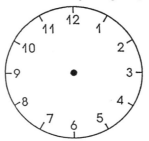 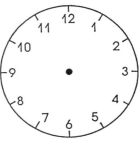

Answer: _____

 IF8746 Math Topics

Name _____

Planning Your Attack

Write your method of solution for each of the following problems. The first one is done for you.

1. If you know the price of a circus ticket and you pay for it with a ten dollar bill, how do you figure the amount of change you will get?

   Subtract the price of the ticket from $10.00.

2. If you know the price of a circus ticket, how do you find the total cost of tickets for you and 2 of your friends?

3. If you know how many clowns are now performing and how many are yet to appear, how do you find the number of clowns in the circus?

4. You know the number of shows the circus performs in a year and the number they have already performed. How do you find the number left to be performed this year?

5. If you know the amount you paid for 3 bags of popcorn, how do you find the cost of one bag?

6. You know the number of animals in the circus. You also know there are four times as many animals as people. How do you find the number of people in the circus?

7. You know the amount of food eaten each day by all the circus animals. How do you find the amount of food the animals eat in a week?

<u>Name</u>

Problem Solving Review — I

Solve the following problems.

1. You weigh 145 pounds, and your space suit weighs 250 pounds. How much would you weigh in all when you climb into your spaceship?

2. Apollo 10 traveled at a speed which was 450 times the speed of a car traveling down the highway at 55 miles per hour. What was the speed of Apollo 10?

3. John Glenn spent a little less than 5 hours in space. Sally Ride spent 14 days and 8 hours in space. How many hours did Sally Ride spend in space?

4. During 2 flights, Owen Garriott spent 69 days in space. Garriott spent 3 times as long in space as did Eugene Cernan. How many days did Cernan spend in space?

5. The space shuttle at liftoff weighs about 4,500,000 pounds. How much heavier is the space shuttle than the earth vehicle you travel in, which weighs around 2,000 pounds?

6. A space orbiter is as tall as a 12-story building. If each of the 12 stories is 14 feet tall, how tall is the orbiter?

7. When the work is done in space and the shuttle re-enters Earth's atmosphere, it gets very hot. The temperature on the nose of the shuttle gets up to 30 times as hot as the temperature here on a 90°F day. How hot is the nose of the shuttle?

<u>Name</u>

Problem Solving Review — II

Solve the following problems.

1. On a clear night you can see about 2,700 stars. In one year you can see some 6,000 different stars. How many more stars would you see in one year than in one night?

2. The exosphere begins at about 250 miles above the Earth and stretches to about 800 miles above Earth. How deep is the exosphere?

3. The distance from the sun to Earth, called one astronomical unit (AU), is 93 million miles. The distance from the sun to Jupiter is 5 AU's. How many miles is it from the sun to Jupiter?

4. Neptune is 30 AU's from the sun. An AU is 93 million miles. How many miles is Neptune from the sun?

5. It is about 3,000 miles across the U.S. It is 80 times that distance from Earth to the Earth's moon. How far is it from Earth to the Earth's moon?

6. A Jupiter year is almost 12 Earth years long. Since our year is 365 days, how many Earth days are there in a Jupiter year?

7. 9 years after Voyager I was launched, it passed Neptune. Voyager I traveled nearly 280 million miles per year. How far did Voyager I travel to get to Neptune?

IF8746 Math Topics

Answer Key

Page 1

Easy Street

Name _____

Easy does it! What is each house worth?
Count the money in each house on Easy
Street. Write the amount on the line.

Example

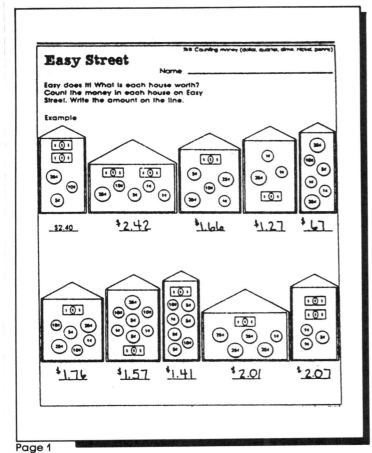

$2.40 $2.42 $1.66 $1.27 $.67

$1.76 $1.57 $1.41 $2.01 $2.07

Page 2

Your Answer's SAFE with Me

Name _____

Find the right "combination" to open each
safe. Draw the bills and coins needed to
make each amount.

Answers will vary.

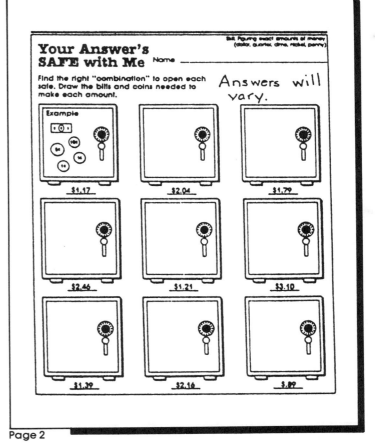

Example

$1.17 $2.04 $1.79

$2.46 $1.21 $3.10

$1.39 $2.16 $.89

Page 3

Coupon Capers

Name _____

Cut the cost with these coupons. Subtract the cents off
from the price. How much do the books cost now?

Example   Work Space

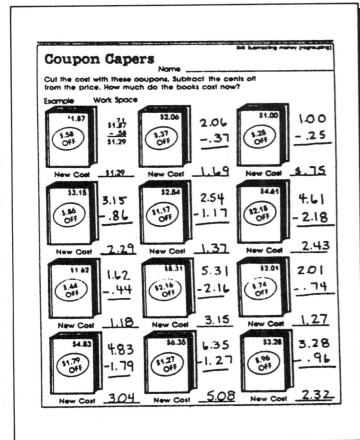

$1.87 $1.87 $2.06   2.06 $1.00   1.00
$.58 OFF   -.58 $.37 OFF -.37 $.25 OFF -.25
           $1.29

New Cost $1.29   New Cost 1.69   New Cost .75

$3.15   3.15 $2.54   2.54 $4.61   4.61
$.86 OFF -.86 $1.17 OFF -1.17 $2.18 OFF -2.18

New Cost 2.29   New Cost 1.37   New Cost 2.43

$1.62   1.62 $5.31   5.31 $2.01   2.01
$.44 OFF -.44 $2.16 OFF -2.16 $.74 OFF -.74

New Cost 1.18   New Cost 3.15   New Cost 1.27

$4.83   4.83 $6.35   6.35 $3.28   3.28
$1.79 OFF -1.79 $1.27 OFF -1.27 $.96 OFF -.96

New Cost 3.04   New Cost 5.08   New Cost 2.32

Page 4

Top "Billing"

Name _____

The spotlight is on you!

Circle the amount you would give the
clerk to buy each hat.

Then subtract to find how much change
you would get.

Example

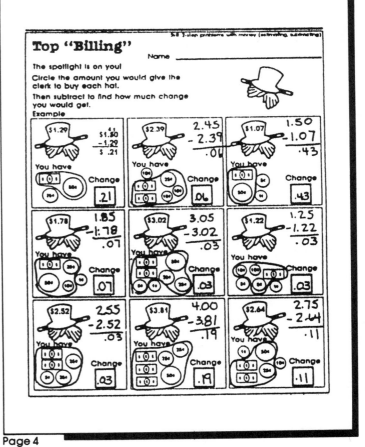

$1.29 $1.50 $2.39   2.45 $1.07   1.50
        -1.29   -2.39   -1.07
        $ .21   .06   .43

You have Change .21   You have Change .06   You have Change .43

$1.78   1.85 $3.02   3.05 $1.22   1.25
        -1.78   -3.02   -1.22
        .07   .03   .03

You have Change .07   You have Change .03   You have Change .03

$2.52   2.55 $3.81   4.00 $2.64   2.75
        -2.52   -3.81   -2.64
        .03   .19   .11

You have Change .03   You have Change .19   You have Change .11

Answer Key

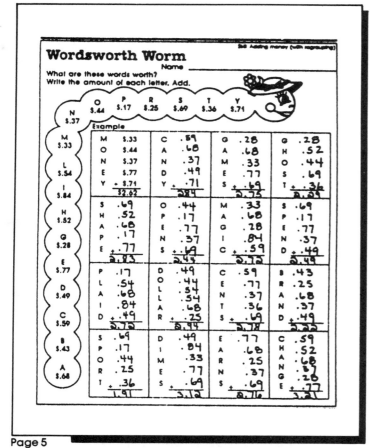

Wordsworth Worm

What are these words worth?
Write the amount of each letter. Add.

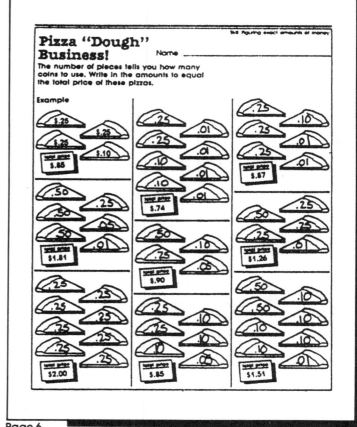

Pizza "Dough" Business!

The number of pieces tells you how many coins to use. Write in the amounts to equal the total price of these pizzas.

Example

One-Stop Shopping

Stash McCash is shopping! Find the total cost of the items. Then find how much change Stash should receive.

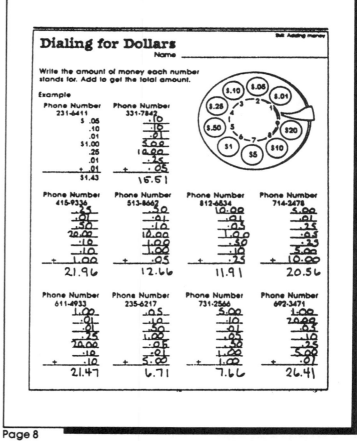

Dialing for Dollars

Write the amount of money each number stands for. Add to get the total amount.

Example

IF8746 Math Topics

Answer Key

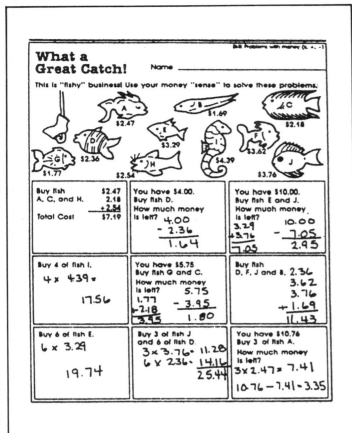

What a Great Catch!

Name _____

This is "fishy" business! Use your money "sense" to solve these problems.

Buy fish $2.47 / A, C, and H. 2.18 / +2.54 / **Total Cost $7.19**	You have $4.00. Buy fish D. How much money is left? 4.00 − 2.36 = 1.64
You have $10.00. Buy fish E and J. How much money is left? 3.29 +3.76 = 7.05 / 10.00 − 7.05 = 2.95	
Buy 4 of fish I. 4 × 4.39 = 17.56	You have $5.75 Buy fish G and C. How much money is left? 5.75 1.77 +2.18 = 3.95 / 5.75 − 3.95 = 1.80
Buy fish D, F, J and B. 2.36 3.62 3.76 +1.69 = 11.43	
Buy 6 of fish E. 6 × 3.29 = 19.74	Buy 3 of fish J and 6 of fish D. 3 × 3.76 = 11.28 / 6 × 2.36 = 14.16 / 25.44
You have $10.76 Buy 3 of fish A. How much money is left? 3 × 2.47 = 7.41 / 10.76 − 7.41 = 3.35	

Page 9

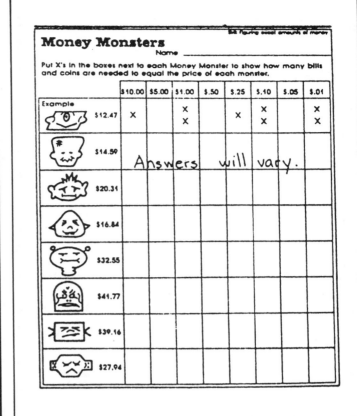

Money Monsters

Name _____

Put X's in the boxes next to each Money Monster to show how many bills and coins are needed to equal the price of each monster.

		$10.00	$5.00	$1.00	$.50	$.25	$.10	$.05	$.01
Example	$12.47	X		X X		X	X X		X X
	$14.59		Answers	will	vary.				
	$20.31								
	$16.84								
	$32.55								
	$41.77								
	$39.16								
	$27.94								

Page 10

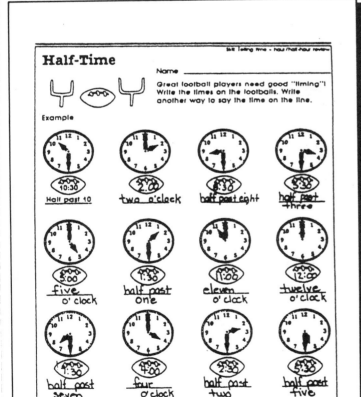

Half-Time

Name _____

Great football players need good "timing"! Write the times on the footballs. Write another way to say the time on the line.

Example: 10:30 — Half past 10

- 2:00 — two o'clock
- 8:30 — half past eight
- 3:30 — half past three
- 5:00 — five o'clock
- 1:30 — half past one
- 11:00 — eleven o'clock
- 12:00 — twelve o'clock
- 7:30 — half past seven
- 4:00 — four o'clock
- 2:30 — half past two
- 5:30 — half past five

Page 11

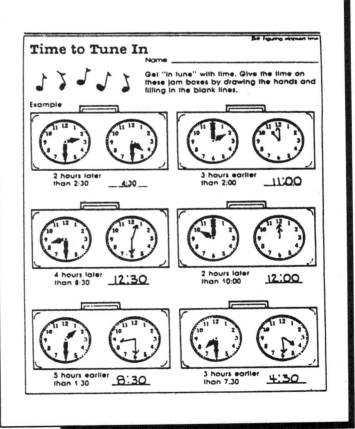

Time to Tune In

Name _____

Get "in tune" with time. Give the time on these jam boxes by drawing the hands and filling in the blank lines.

Example:

- 2 hours later than 2:30 — 4:30
- 3 hours earlier than 2:00 — 11:00
- 4 hours later than 8:30 — 12:30
- 2 hours later than 10:00 — 12:00
- 5 hours earlier than 1:30 — 8:30
- 3 hours earlier than 7:30 — 4:30

Page 12

Answer Key

Missing Hands

Name _____

The minute hands are missing on these clocks. Can you still tell what hour or half hour the clocks show? Write the time on the line and draw the missing minute hand.

(Hint: If the time is exactly on the hour, then the hour hand is exactly on the number. If the time is on the half hour, then the minute hand is half way between the numbers.)

Example

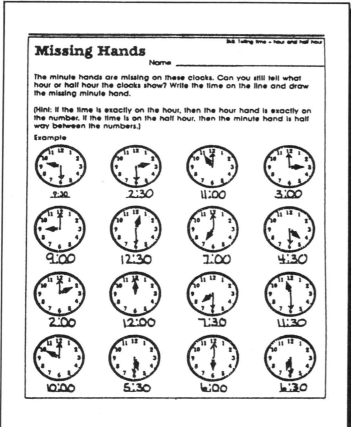

Row 1: 9:30 2:30 11:00 3:00
Row 2: 9:00 12:30 1:00 4:30
Row 3: 2:00 12:00 7:30 11:30
Row 4: 10:00 5:30 6:00 6:30

Pizza Time

Name _____

Chef "Time-It-Right" is baking pizzas. Can you help him fill in his timing schedule?

In the Oven	Baking Time	Out of the Oven
Example 6:00	1/2 hour	6:30
8:30	2 hours	10:30
4:30	1 hour	5:30
9:00	1 hour	10:00
1:30	2 1/2 hours	4:00
5:00	1½ hours	6:30
3:00	1 hour	4:00
12:00	2 1/2 hours	2:30
7:00	1/2 hour	7:30
8:00	1½ hours	9:30
2:30	1 1/2 hours	4:00
11:00	3 hours	2:00
3:30	1½ hours	5:00

Page 13

Page 14

Solar Scholars

Name _____

Keep your sunny side up! Write the time.

Example

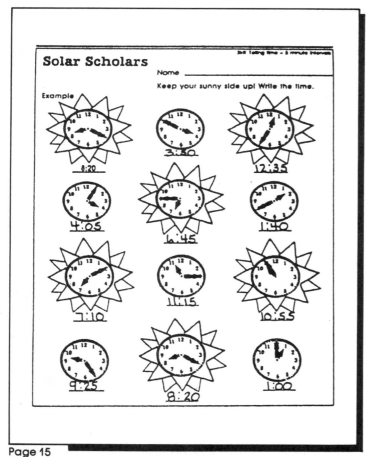

8:20   3:30   12:35
4:05   6:45   1:40
7:10   11:15   10:55
9:25   8:20   1:00

Time On My Hands

Name _____

Draw the hour and minute hands.

Example

Row 1: 3:35 10:05 4:55 8:10
Row 2: 12:50 9:20 7:25 1:15
Row 3: 11:45 3:30 6:40 12:55
Row 4: 2:00 5:35 3:15 10:50

Page 15

Page 16

IF8746 Math Topics

Answer Key

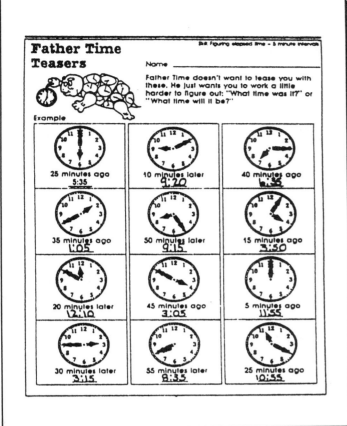

Father Time Teasers

Name _____

Father Time doesn't want to tease you with these. He just wants you to work a little harder to figure out: "What time was it?" or "What time will it be?"

Example

25 minutes ago 5:35	10 minutes later 9:20	40 minutes ago 10:35
35 minutes ago 1:05	50 minutes later 9:15	15 minutes ago 3:50
20 minutes later 12:10	45 minutes ago 3:05	5 minutes ago 11:55
30 minutes later 3:15	55 minutes later 8:35	25 minutes ago 10:55

Page 17

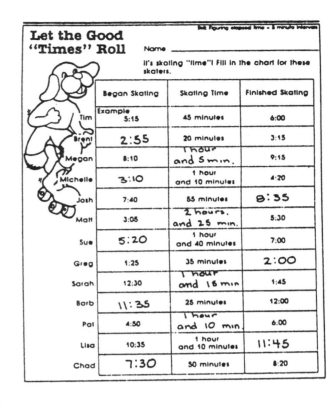

Let the Good "Times" Roll

Name _____

It's skating "time"! Fill in the chart for these skaters.

	Began Skating	Skating Time	Finished Skating
Tim	Example 5:15	45 minutes	6:00
Brent	2:55	20 minutes	3:15
Megan	8:10	1 hour and 5 min.	9:15
Michelle	3:10	1 hour and 10 minutes	4:20
Josh	7:40	55 minutes	8:35
Matt	3:05	2 hours and 25 min.	5:30
Sue	5:20	1 hour and 40 minutes	7:00
Greg	1:25	35 minutes	2:00
Sarah	12:30	1 hour and 15 min	1:45
Barb	11:35	25 minutes	12:00
Pat	4:50	1 hour and 10 min.	6:00
Lisa	10:35	1 hour and 10 minutes	11:45
Chad	7:30	50 minutes	8:20

Page 18

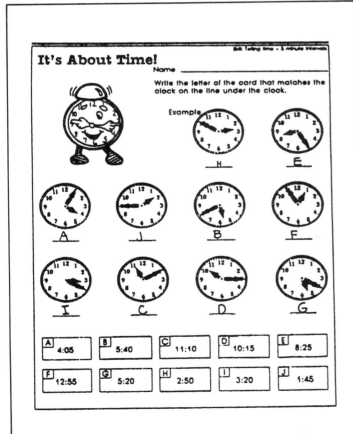

It's About Time!

Name _____

Write the letter of the card that matches the clock on the line under the clock.

Example
H   E
A   J   B   F
I   C   D   G

| A | 4:05 | B | 5:40 | C | 11:10 | D | 10:15 | E | 8:25 |
| F | 12:55 | G | 5:20 | H | 2:50 | I | 3:20 | J | 1:45 |

Page 19

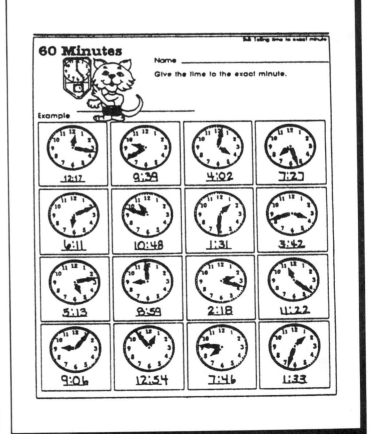

60 Minutes

Name _____

Give the time to the exact minute.

Example

12:17	9:38	4:02	7:27
6:11	10:48	1:31	3:42
5:13	8:59	2:18	11:22
9:06	12:54	7:46	1:33

Page 20

IF8746 Math Topics

Answer Key

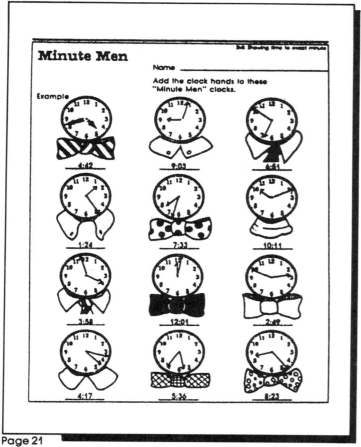

Minute Men

Name _____

Add the clock hands to these "Minute Men" clocks.

Example

4:42   9:03   6:51

1:24   7:33   10:11

3:58   12:01   2:49

4:17   5:36   8:23

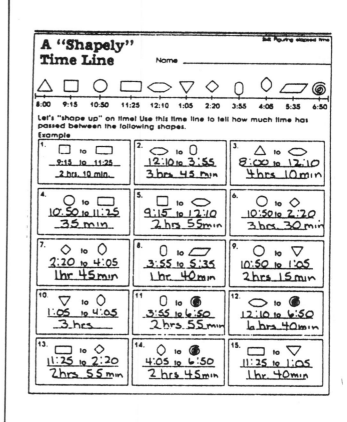

A "Shapely" Time Line

Name _____

8:00 9:15 10:50 11:25 12:10 1:05 2:20 3:55 4:05 5:35 6:50

Let's "shape up" on time! Use this time line to tell how much time has passed between the following shapes.

Example

1. ☐ to ☐	2. ◇ to ◯	3. △ to ◇
9:15 to 11:25	12:10 to 3:55	8:00 to 12:10
2 hrs. 10 min.	3 hrs 45 min	4 hrs 10 min
4. ◯ to ☐	5. ☐ to ◇	6. ◯ to ◇
10:50 to 11:25	9:15 to 12:10	10:50 to 2:20
35 min	2 hrs 55min	3 hrs 30 min
7. ◇ to ◯	8. ◯ to ▱	9. ◯ to ▽
2:20 to 4:05	3:55 to 5:35	10:50 to 1:05
1hr 45min	1 hr 40 min	2hrs 15min
10. ◯ to ◯	11. ◯ to ◉	12. ◇ to ◉
1:05 to 4:05	3:55 to 6:50	12:10 to 6:50
3 hrs	2 hrs 55 min	6 hrs 40 min
13. ☐ to ◇	14. ◇ to ◉	15. ☐ to ▽
11:25 to 2:20	4:05 to 6:50	11:25 to 1:05
2hrs 55 min	2 hrs 45min	1hr. 40min

Time "Tables"

Name _____

"Set" these tables by drawing the hands to these clocks.

Example

10 minutes before   36 minutes after   8 minutes before
12:17   8:19   1:08

21 minutes after   16 minutes before   46 minutes after
8:40   4:30   10:11

32 minutes before   11 minutes after   24 minutes before
5:25   3:16   12:30

17 minutes after   43 minutes before   18 minutes after
1:31   2:01   6:45

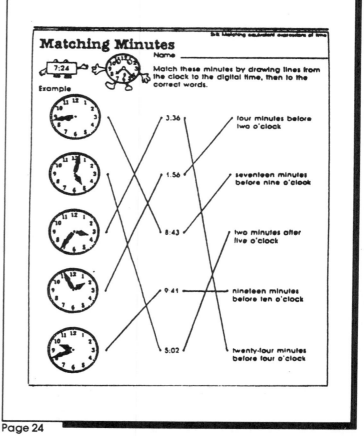

Matching Minutes

Name _____

7:24

Match these minutes by drawing lines from the clock to the digital time, then to the correct words.

Example

3:36   four minutes before two o'clock

1:56   seventeen minutes before nine o'clock

8:43   two minutes after five o'clock

9:41   nineteen minutes before ten o'clock

5:02   twenty-four minutes before four o'clock

Answer Key

Minute Maid!
How long does it take the "Minute Maid" to do her household tasks?

	Time Started	Length of Task	Time Ended
Polishing	Example 9:14	35 minutes	9:49
Dusting	7:18	42 minutes	8:00
Waxing	10:03	48 min.	10:51
Mopping	2:36	29 minutes	3:05
Cleaning Windows	4:45	47 min.	5:32
Serving Breakfast	7:12	18 minutes	7:30
Laundry	11:10	58 minutes	12:08
Ironing	12:13	47 min.	1:00
Serving Lunch	11:30	24 minutes	11:54
Vacuuming	3:16	41 minutes	3:57
Serving Dinner	5:30	27 min.	5:57
Hanging Curtains	6:26	56 minutes	7:22
Making Beds	8:03	38 min.	8:41

Page 25

It's High-Time!

A.M. is the time after 12:00 midnight and before 12:00 noon.
P.M. is the time after 12:00 noon and before 12:00 midnight.
Write A.M. or P.M. for these events.

Example
1. The sun sets. P.M.
2. You get up. A.M.
3. You eat dinner. P.M.
4. Afternoon P.M.
5. The sun rises. A.M.
6. Morning cartoons A.M.
7. You have lunch. P.M. (varies)
8. Evening P.M.
9. Afternoon soccer P.M.
10. You eat breakfast. A.M.
11. Morning exercises A.M.
12. Evening TV shows P.M.
13. Evening piano class P.M.
14. Morning music class A.M.
15. Home from school P.M.
16. Afternoon art class P.M.
17. Catch morning bus A.M.
18. After-school snack P.M.
19. You go to bed. P.M.
20. Morning gym A.M.
21. Before school jobs A.M.
22. Evening dance class P.M.
23. Afternoon Reading P.M.
24. Morning snack A.M.

Page 26

Take Time for These . . .

Be right on time! Write the exact time shown on these clocks.

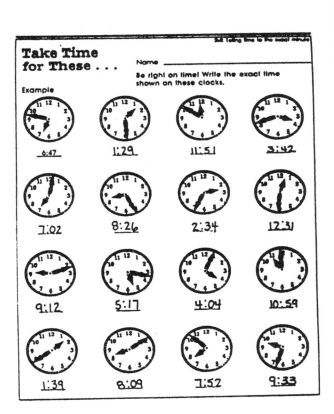

Example
6:47   1:29   11:51   3:42
7:02   8:26   2:34   12:31
9:12   5:17   4:04   10:59
1:39   8:09   7:52   9:33

Page 27

Minute Monsters

The Minute Monsters have their pairs of shoes mixed up. Cut out the shoes. Glue the matching pairs onto another paper.

1 hr. 15 min. after 6:20 — 7:35 | 6:50
2 hrs. 5 min. after 1:10 — 3:15 | 8:00
48 min. after 2:35 — 3:20 | 8:20
2 hrs. 10 min. before 4:00 — 1:50 | 7:35
3 hrs. 10 min. before 10:00 — 6:50 | 2:20
1 hr. 50 min. before 6:10 — 4:20 | 2:30
45 min. before 1:45 — 2:30 | 4:20
55 min. before 3:15 — 2:20 | 3:45
1 hr. 25 min. before 9:45 — 8:20 | 1:50
2 hrs. 35 min. after 5:25 — 8:00 | 3:15
1 hr. 10 min. before 12:00 — 10:50 | 3:20
3 hrs. 15 min. before 7:00 — 3:45 | 10:50

Page 28

©1992 Instructional Fair, Inc.   109   IF8746 Math Topics

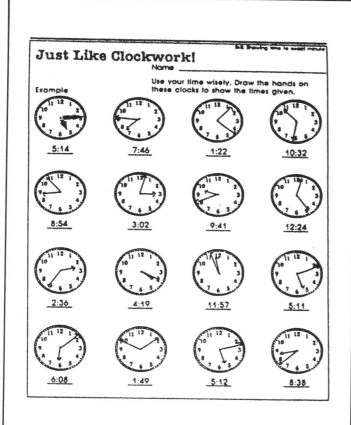

Just Like Clockwork!

Name _____

Example

Use your time wisely. Draw the hands on these clocks to show the times given.

5:14   7:46   1:22   10:32

8:54   3:02   9:41   12:24

2:36   4:19   11:57   5:11

6:08   1:49   5:12   8:38

Page 29

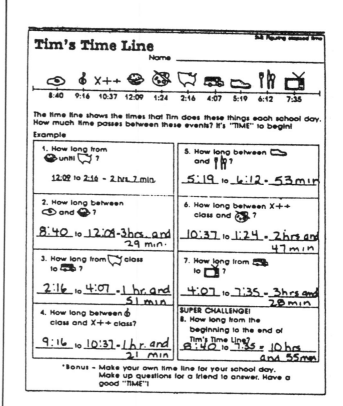

Tim's Time Line

Name _____

8:40   9:16   10:37   12:09   1:24   2:16   4:07   5:19   6:12   7:35

The time line shows the times that Tim does these things each school day. How much time passes between these events? It's "TIME" to begin!

Example

1. How long from ⬤ until 🇺🇸 ?
12:09 to 2:16 = 2 hrs. 7 min.

2. How long between ⬤ and 🌍 ?
8:40 to 12:09 = 3 hrs. and 29 min.

3. How long from 🇺🇸 class to 🚐 ?
2:16 to 4:07 = 1 hr. and 51 min

4. How long between 🔔 class and X++ class?
9:16 to 10:37 = 1 hr. and 21 min

5. How long between 👟 and 🍴 ?
5:19 to 6:12 = 53 min

6. How long between X++ class and 🌍 ?
10:37 to 1:24 = 2 hrs and 47 min

7. How long from 🚐 to 📺 ?
4:07 to 7:35 = 3 hrs and 28 min

SUPER CHALLENGE!
8. How long from the beginning to the end of Tim's Time Line?
8:40 to 7:35 = 10 hrs and 55 min

*Bonus – Make your own time line for your school day. Make up questions for a friend to answer. Have a good "TIME"!

Page 30

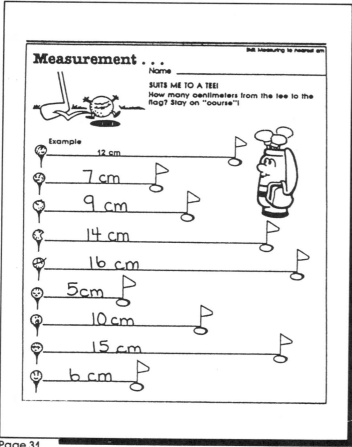

Measurement . . .

Name _____

SUITS ME TO A TEE!
How many centimeters from the tee to the flag? Stay on "course"!

Example
12 cm

7 cm

9 cm

14 cm

16 cm

5 cm

10 cm

15 cm

6 cm

Page 31

Batter Up!

Name _____

1. How many centimeters from homeplate to first base? 8

2. The ball in left field is 7 cm from the pitcher's mound. Measure from ★.

3. How far is it from the pitcher's mound to homeplate? 4 cm Measure from ★.

4. The ball in right field is 11 cm from homeplate. Measure from ★.

5. A throw from third base to first base would be 14 cm long.

⊗   2nd   ⊗

3rd 1st

H

Page 32

Answer Key

Sawing Logs

Name _____

Measure the logs to the nearest centimeter.

Example

8 cm

15 cm

11 cm

9 cm

14 cm

7 cm

16 cm

Luck of the Draw!

Name _____

1. In Box A, draw a pencil that is 15 cm long (from the widest part of the eraser to the pencil point). The pencil is 2 cm wide. Color and write your name on it.

2. In Box B, draw a rectangle that is 7 cm long and 4 cm wide. Decorate it as a birthday present.

3. In Box C, draw a triangle with all three sides 4 cm long. Put a point toward the top and make it into a funny oar.

Box A

Box B

Box C

The Metric Kingdom

Name _____

Visit the Metric Amusement Park by measuring the distance to these attractions. Measure from ★ to ★.

1. The Fantastic Ferris Wheel is __13__ cm from Dandy's Dart Booth.

2. The beach ball is __8__ cm from Barney, the Balloon Man.

3. The Centimeter Streak Roller Coaster is __7__ cm from the Fantastic Ferris Wheel.

4. The antique car is __4__ cm from Barney, the Balloon Man.

5. The Centimeter Sailor Sailboat is __10__ cm from the roller coaster.

6. Dandy's Dart Booth is __4__ cm from Gram's Bell Ringer Booth.

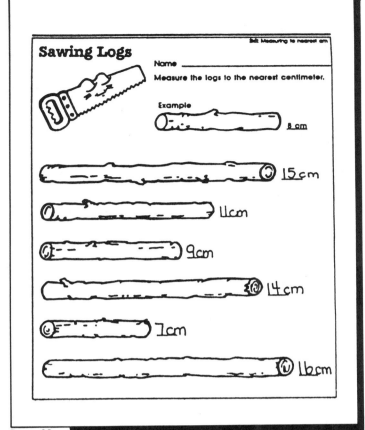

Ella Elephant

Name _____

Read the picture graph. Answer the questions.

Monday
Tuesday
Wednesday
Thursday
Friday

1. How many butterflies did Ella Elephant catch on Monday? _2_ Tuesday? _5_ Wednesday? _3_ Thursday? _6_ Friday _4_ ?

2. On what day did she catch the most? __Thursday__ Color them blue.

3. On what day did she catch the least? __Monday__ Color them red.

4. How many butterflies did Ella catch in all? __20__

5. Draw a green ☐ around the best day to catch butterflies.

IF8746 Math Topics

Flower Graph

Skill: Making a picture bar graph (counting and comparing)

Name _____

Cut out and match the flowers to the graph.

Daisies						
Sunflowers						
Tulips						
Roses						

How many tulips? _5_ Sunflowers? _3_ Roses? _2_ Daisies? _4_
How many more tulips than roses? _3_
How many more daisies than sunflowers? _1_
How many sunflowers and tulips? _8_
How many roses and daisies? _6_

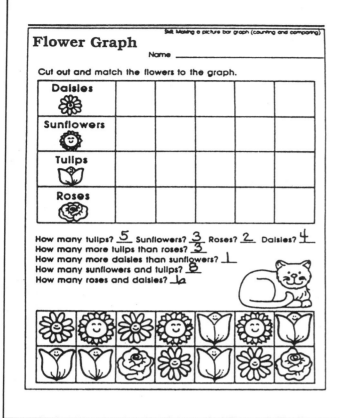

Potato Face

Skill: Reading line graphs

Name _____

Read the line graphs to draw the potato faces.

How many?
👁's _1_ 👂's _4_ 😀's _2_ 👃's _3_

How many?
👁's _4_ 👂's _2_ 😀's _3_ 👃's _1_

Frog Bubbles

Skill: Drawing a line graph

Name _____

Color the picture.

Finish the line graph to show how many bubbles.

	Frog 1	Frog 2	Frog 3	Frog 4	Frog 5
5					
4					
3					
2					
1					

How many bubbles? Frog 1? _3_ 2? _5_ 3? _4_ 4? _1_ 5? _4_
Which frog blew the most bubbles? _2_ Which frog blew the least? _4_

Lizzy the Lizard

Skill: One-Step Problems with Addition (Review of Facts)

Name _____

Lizzy the Lizard has a great collection of insects. She is always on the lookout for new and different types of bugs.

1. Lizzy collected 5 ants and 6 beetles in a morning. What was the sum?

$5 + 6 = 11$

2. Lizzy the Lizard caught 11 crickets and 7 grasshoppers in an evening. How many insects did she catch in all?

$11 + 7 = 18$

3. Lizzy found 7 bees and 8 wasps on a tour of her garden. How many insects did she find?

$7 + 8 = 15$

4. Lizzy and her brother Dizzy found 7 stinkbugs and 6 lice on Sunday. How many insects did they find altogether?

$7 + 6 = 13$

5. Lizzy caught 7 mud wasps. Izzy caught 6 waterbugs. Dizzy caught 4 flies. How many bugs did they catch in all?

$7 + 6 + 4 = 17$

6. Lizzy found 9 ants in the morning and 9 more ants in afternoon. How many ants did she find in all?

$9 + 9 = 18$

 IF8746 Math Topics

Answer Key

Suzy D. Spider

Name _____

1. Suzy D. Spider has 8 legs. Her friend Ant Betty has 6 legs. How many more legs does Suzy have?

$$8 - 6 = 2$$

2. Suzy caught 16 flies in a week. The next week she caught only 9 flies. What was the difference?

$$16 - 9 = 7$$

3. Suzy had 15 children. 9 of them were boys. How many were girls?

$$15 - 9 = 6$$

4. Suzy scared 11 people on Sunday. She scared only 6 people on Monday. What was the difference?

$$11 - 6 = 5$$

5. Suzy is 16 millimeters long. Her sister is 11 millimeters long. How much longer is Suzy?

$$16 \text{ mm} - 11 \text{ mm} = 5 \text{ mm}$$

6. Suzy trapped 17 flies in her web. Her sister Sally trapped 8 flies. How many more did Suzy trap?

$$17 - 8 = 9$$

7. Suzy D. Spider ate 12 mealworms and 18 fruit flies in a week. How many more fruit flies did she eat?

$$18 - 12 = 6$$

Page 41

The Missing Teeth

Name _____

1. Cal Coyote had 42 teeth. He lost 11 teeth. How many does he have left?

$$\begin{array}{r} 42 \\ -11 \\ \hline 31 \end{array}$$

2. Roger Raccoon had 40 teeth before 10 fell out. How many does he have left?

$$\begin{array}{r} 40 \\ -10 \\ \hline 30 \end{array}$$

3. Harry House Mouse used to have 16 teeth. He now has 11 teeth. How many of his teeth has he lost?

$$\begin{array}{r} 16 \\ -11 \\ \hline 5 \end{array}$$

4. Red Fox has 31 teeth now. He used to have 42 teeth. How many did he lose?

$$\begin{array}{r} 42 \\ -31 \\ \hline 11 \end{array}$$

5. Peter Possum used to have 50 teeth. The busy tooth fairy has paid him for 40 teeth. How many teeth does Peter have left?

$$\begin{array}{r} 50 \\ -40 \\ \hline 10 \end{array}$$

6. Slinky the Skunk has 12 teeth. He used to have 34. How many of his teeth has he lost?

$$\begin{array}{r} 34 \\ -12 \\ \hline 22 \end{array}$$

7. Woody Woodchuck now has 11 teeth. He used to have 22 teeth. How many has he lost?

$$\begin{array}{r} 22 \\ -11 \\ \hline 11 \end{array}$$

Page 42

McMealworm

Name _____

McMealworm's is the latest restaurant of that famous fast food creator, Buggs I. Lyke. His McMealworm Burger costs $1.69. An order of Roasted Roaches costs $.59 for the regular size and $.79 for the large size. A Cricket Cola is $.89.

1. You buy a McMealworm Burger and a regular order of Roasted Roaches. What is the total?

$$\begin{array}{r} \$1.69 \\ +.59 \\ \hline \$2.28 \end{array}$$

2. Your best friend in class orders a McMealworm Burger, a large order of Roasted Roaches and a Cricket Cola. How much will it cost?

$$\begin{array}{r} \$1.69 \\ .79 \\ +.89 \\ \hline \$3.37 \end{array}$$

3. Your teacher buys a Cricket Cola and a regular order of Roasted Roaches. What does it cost?

$$\begin{array}{r} \$.89 \\ +.59 \\ \hline \$1.48 \end{array}$$

4. The principal is very hungry, so his bill comes to $14.37. How much change will he get from $20.00?

$$\begin{array}{r} \$20.00 \\ -14.37 \\ \hline \$5.63 \end{array}$$

5. Your mom goes to McMealworm's to buy your dinner. She spends $3.37. How much change does she get from a $5.00 bill?

$$\begin{array}{r} \$5.00 \\ -3.37 \\ \hline \$1.63 \end{array}$$

6. You have $1.17 in your bank. How much more do you need to pay for a McMealworm Burger?

$$\begin{array}{r} \$1.69 \\ -1.17 \\ \hline \$.52 \end{array}$$

Page 43

Wacky Waldo's Animal Circus

Name _____

Wacky Waldo has trained a very unusual animal circus. He has taught sharks to ride tricycles. He has trained mice to scare tigers and snakes to be as cuddly as kittens. He has even trained donkeys to fly like sparrows.

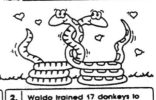

1. Wacky Waldo taught 15 sharks to ride tricycles and 34 mice to scare tigers. How many more mice has he taught?

$$\begin{array}{r} 34 \\ -15 \\ \hline 19 \end{array}$$

2. Waldo trained 17 donkeys to fly through the air like little birds. He also taught 18 snakes to cuddle up like little kittens. How many animals were trained altogether?

$$\begin{array}{r} 17 \\ +18 \\ \hline 35 \end{array}$$

3. Waldo had trained 45 flying donkeys. One night 26 donkeys flew away. How many donkeys were left?

$$\begin{array}{r} 45 \\ -26 \\ \hline 19 \end{array}$$

4. Wacky has 112 flies who have been taught to bite fish and 98 flies who have been taught to chase frogs. What is the total?

$$\begin{array}{r} 112 \\ +98 \\ \hline 210 \end{array}$$

5. One evening, 69 sharks rode tricycles. On the same night, 46 whales rode bicycles. How many animals were riding that night?

$$\begin{array}{r} 69 \\ +46 \\ \hline 115 \end{array}$$

6. On Sunday, 56 snakes learned to be warm and cuddly. On Monday, 38 more snakes learned how to cuddle up. How many more snakes were trained on Sunday?

$$\begin{array}{r} 56 \\ -38 \\ \hline 18 \end{array}$$

Page 44

Answer Key

Page 45

Percy P. Porcupine

Skill: One-Step Problems with Addition and Subtraction (Regrouping)

Name _____

Percy P. Porcupine created a sensation one morning when he decided to go to school to get an education.

To School

1. Percy met 19 dogs and 12 cats on the way to school, but none of them wanted to play with him. How many animals did he meet?

$$\begin{array}{r} 19 \\ +12 \\ \hline 31 \end{array}$$

2. Percy had a disagreement with the school bully. The bully got 64 quills in his right hand and 56 in his left. How many more quills were in his right hand?

$$\begin{array}{r} 5\,6\,4 \\ -56 \\ \hline 8 \end{array}$$

3. A kindergarten teacher thought Percy was cute and tried to pet him. She got 37 quills stuck in her hand. She got 18 out. How many were still in her hand?

$$\begin{array}{r} 2\,37 \\ -18 \\ \hline 19 \end{array}$$

4. Percy visited the third grade classroom and counted 16 boys and 17 girls. What was the sum?

$$\begin{array}{r} 1\,6 \\ +17 \\ \hline 33 \end{array}$$

5. A dog named Bow-Wow tried to rub noses with Percy. He got 27 quills in his nose and 16 in his neck. How many quills did he get in all?

$$\begin{array}{r} 27 \\ +16 \\ \hline 43 \end{array}$$

6. Percy visited the principal. He gave him 26 quills. He gave the secretary 35 quills. How many more quills did the secretary get?

$$\begin{array}{r} 2\,35 \\ -26 \\ \hline 9 \end{array}$$

Page 46

Beetle in a Box

Skill: Working with Money (Addition and Subtraction with Regrouping)

Name _____

A brand-new fast food place called Beetle In a Box has opened up near your school. You can buy a Beetle Burger for $1.39, Fried Flies for $.79 and a Cocoon Cola for $.98.

CAT RAT

6×6=36

1. You order a Beetle Burger and a Cocoon Cola on your way home from school. How much will they cost?

$$\begin{array}{r} \$1.39 \\ +\ .98 \\ \hline \$2.37 \end{array}$$

2. Your teacher wants a snack after school. She orders Fried Flies and a Cocoon Cola. What is the total?

$$\begin{array}{r} \$\ .79 \\ .98 \\ \hline \$1.77 \end{array}$$

3. You and your family had dinner at Beetle In a Box. The bill was $15.78. Your father gave the waitress a $20.00 bill. How much change should he have received?

$$\begin{array}{r} \$20.00 \\ -15.78 \\ \hline \$\ 4.22 \end{array}$$

4. Jamie gave the owner a $10.00 bill to pay for an order that cost $4.14. How much change did he get?

$$\begin{array}{r} \$10.00 \\ -\ 4.14 \\ \hline \$\ 5.86 \end{array}$$

5. How much will it cost you for a Beetle Burger and Fried Flies?

$$\begin{array}{r} \$1.39 \\ +\ .79 \\ \hline \$2.18 \end{array}$$

6. The nearest hamburger stand sells beef burgers for $1.88. How much less is a Beetle Burger?

$$\begin{array}{r} \$1.88 \\ -1.39 \\ \hline \$\ .49 \end{array}$$

Page 47

Mean Monster's Multiplication

Skill: One-Step Problems with Multiplication Facts

Name _____

Mean Monster is a football player for the Oki Doki Outlaws. He weighs over 400 pounds and is 7 feet tall. He is not a good student. He spent 3 years in first grade. He thinks there are only 24 letters in the alphabet because he thinks P's and B's are something to eat.

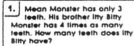

1. Mean Monster has only 3 teeth. His brother Itty Bitty Monster has 4 times as many teeth. How many teeth does Itty Bitty have?

$3 \times 4 = 12$

2. Mean Monster learned 6 letters in kindergarten. He learned 3 times as many in first grade. How many did he learn in first grade?

$6 \times 3 = 18$

3. Mean Monster ate 5 sandwiches for lunch on Thursday. He ate 4 times as many sandwiches on Friday. How many sandwiches did he eat on Friday?

$5 \times 4 = 20$

4. Mean Monster ate 5 P's. He ate 6 times as many B's. How many B's did he eat?

$5 \times 6 = 30$

5. In the first play of the game, Mean Monster gained 7 yards. On the next play, he gained 4 times as many yards. How many yards did he gain on the second play?

$7 \times 4 = 28$

6. Itty Bitty Monster broke 2 fingers trying to catch a coconut. Mean Monster broke 5 times as many fingers trying to catch a brick. How many fingers did Mean Monster break?

$2 \times 5 = 10$

Page 48

Wacky Waldo's Snow Show

Skill: One-Step Problems with Multiplication Facts

Name _____

Wacky Waldo's Snow Show is an exciting and fantastic sight. Waldo has trained whales and bears to skate together on the ice. There is a hockey game between a team of sharks and a pack of wolves. Elephants ride sleds down steep hills. Horses and buffaloes ski swiftly down mountains.

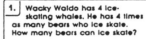

1. Wacky Waldo has 4 ice-skating whales. He has 4 times as many bears who ice skate. How many bears can ice skate?

$4 \times 4 = 16$

2. Waldo's Snow Show has 4 shows on Thursday, but it has 6 times as many shows on Saturday. How many shows are there on Saturday?

$4 \times 6 = 24$

3. The Sharks' hockey team has 3 white sharks. It has 6 times as many tiger sharks. How many tiger sharks does it have?

$3 \times 6 = 18$

4. The Wolves' hockey team has 4 gray wolves. It has 8 times as many red wolves. How many red wolves does it have?

$4 \times 8 = 32$

5. Waldo taught 6 buffaloes to ski. He was able to teach 5 times as many horses to ski. How many horses did he teach?

$6 \times 5 = 30$

6. Buff, a skiing buffalo, took 7 nasty spills when he was learning to ski. His friend Harry Horse fell down 8 times as often. How many times did Harry fall?

$7 \times 8 = 56$

Answer Key

Bob Z. Cat
Skill One-Step Problems with Multiplication (Review of Facts)

Name _____

Bob Z. Cat is a very strange cat. He is terrified of mice and his best friends are dogs. He loves to read when he takes a bubble bath.

1. Bob Z. Cat ran away from 3 mice on Saturday. On Sunday, he ran away from 6 times as many mice. How many did he run from on Sunday?

$3 \times 6 = 18$

2. Bob eats 7 cans of tuna fish in a week. How many cans would he eat in 5 weeks?

$7 \times 5 = 35$

3. Bob Cat loves to read books. Last week he read 4 books. This week he has read 9 times as many. How many has he read this week?

$4 \times 9 = 36$

4. Bob read 4 mystery stories one day and 7 times as many the next day. How many mysteries did he read the second day?

$4 \times 7 = 28$

5. Bob Z. Cat spent only 9 minutes in his bath yesterday. Today he spent 9 times as long relaxing in his bubble bath. How long did he bathe today?

$9 \times 9 = 81$

6. Bob Z. Cat can purr 9 times a minute. How many times can he purr in 8 minutes?

$9 \times 8 = 72$

Page 49

Lizzy the Lizard — Brave Explorer
Skill One-Step Problems with Multiplication (Ten as a Factor)

Name _____

1. Lizzy the Lizard went exploring through the woods. She saw 60 red ants. She saw 5 times as many black ants. How many black ants did she see?

$60 \times 5 = 300$

2. Lizzy counted 40 snails in a field. She counted 7 times as many in a garden. How many were in the garden?

$40 \times 7 = 280$

3. Lizzy found a tree full of termites. She ate only 30 termites, but she counted 7 times as many of them. How many termites did she count?

$30 \times 7 = 210$

4. Lizzy counted 90 bees in a flower bed. She was chased by 6 times as many bees when she accidentally found their hive. How many bees chased her?

$90 \times 6 = 540$

5. Lizzy counted 40 porcupine quills in an hour. She counted 6 times as many quills in a day. How many quills did she count in a day?

$40 \times 6 = 240$

6. Lizzy counted 50 caterpillars on an apple tree and 7 times as many on a peach tree. How many were on the peach tree?

$50 \times 7 = 350$

7. Lizzy discovered a nest of crickets. She ate 20 of them and left 8 times as many. How many did she leave?

$20 \times 8 = 160$

Page 50

Shifty Sam's Shop
Skill Working with Money (Multiplication)

Name _____

Shifty Sam's store is a messy jumble of things. Anything a child could want is there if it can be found under the piles of junk and stuff. But be careful if you buy anything. Check Sam's multiplication!

1. Mighty Man comics cost 13¢ at Shifty Sam's. You buy 4 of these comics. How much should you pay?

$\begin{array}{r} \$.13 \\ \times\ 4 \\ \hline \$.52 \end{array}$

2. Your sister decides to buy 2 copies of the latest hit record by the Bird Brains. Each copy costs 89¢. How much will she pay?

$\begin{array}{r} \$.89 \\ \times\ 2 \\ \hline \$1.78 \end{array}$

3. Your best friend bought 9 marbles at Shifty's. Each marble cost 19¢. How much money did he spend?

$\begin{array}{r} \$.19 \\ \times\ 9 \\ \hline \$1.71 \end{array}$

4. Crazy stickers cost 21¢ each at Sam's. You buy 7 of them. How much should you pay?

$\begin{array}{r} \$.21 \\ \times\ 7 \\ \hline \$1.47 \end{array}$

5. Baseball cards are 11¢ each at Shifty Sam's. How much will it cost you for 8 cards?

$\begin{array}{r} \$.11 \\ \times\ 8 \\ \hline \$.88 \end{array}$

6. Slinky Stickers have a skunk odor. Your best friend bought 7 Slinky Stickers which cost 18¢ each. How much did he spend?

$\begin{array}{r} \$.18 \\ \times\ 7 \\ \hline \$1.26 \end{array}$

Page 51

Molly Mugwumps
Skill One-Step Problems with Multiplication (Larger Factors)

Name _____

Molly Mugwumps is the toughest kid in school. She picks fights with kindergarteners and spends more time in the office than the principal does.

1. Molly is the toughest football player in her school. She ran for 23 yards on one play and went 3 times as far on the next play. How far did she run the second time?

$23\text{yd.} \times 3 = 69\text{yd.}$

2. Molly keeps a rock collection. She has 31 rocks in one sack. She has 7 times as many under her bed. How many rocks are under her bed?

$31 \times 7 = 217$

3. Molly had 42 marbles when she came to school. She went home with 4 times as many. How many did she go home with?

$42 \times 4 = 168$

4. Molly stuffed 21 sticks of gum in her mouth in the morning. In the afternoon, she crammed 9 times as many sticks into her mouth. How many sticks did she have in the afternoon?

$21 \times 9 = 189$

5. Molly got 51 problems wrong in math last week. This week she missed 8 times as many. How many did she miss this week?

$51 \times 8 = 408$

6. Molly was sent to the office 21 days last year. This year she was sent 7 times as often. How many days did she go this year?

$21 \times 7 = 147$

Page 52

Answer Key

Page 53

Bargain Bonanza at Pat's Pet Place

Skill: One-Step Problems with Division (One-Digit Divisors)

Name _____

Pat is having a gigantic sale at his place. Help him divide his animals into groups for the sale.

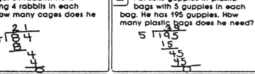

1. Pat got 84 rabbits. He is putting 4 rabbits in each cage. How many cages does he need?

$$\frac{21}{4\overline{)84}}$$
8
4
4

2. Pat sells guppies in plastic bags with 5 guppies in each bag. He has 195 guppies. How many plastic bags does he need?

$$\frac{39}{5\overline{)195}}$$
15
45
45

3. Pat has 392 white mice. They are kept in cages of 7 mice each. How many cages does Pat need?

$$\frac{56}{7\overline{)392}}$$
35
42
42
0

4. Pat has 324 goldfish. If he puts 6 goldfish in each bag, how many plastic bags will he need?

$$\frac{54}{6\overline{)324}}$$
30
24
24
0

5. Pat received 116 hamsters. He keeps them in cages of 4 each. How many cages does he need for his hamsters?

$$\frac{29}{4\overline{)116}}$$
8
36
36
0

6. Pat has 120 parrots. They live in bird cages with 3 to each cage. How many bird cages does Pat need?

$$\frac{40}{3\overline{)120}}$$
12
0

Page 54

Wacky Waldo's Insect Business

Skill: One-Step Multiplication Problems (1 digit × 2 digits)

Name _____

Wacky Waldo, world famous animal trainer, has trained insects to do all kinds of work. He has taught ants to carry bricks and grasshoppers to sing "Yankee Doodle." Cockroaches have been taught to cut hair, and flies have been taught to paint houses.

1. A cockroach can give 9 haircuts in a day. How many haircuts can 31 cockroaches give?

$$\begin{array}{r} 31 \\ \times\ 9 \\ \hline 279 \end{array}$$

2. An ant can put 8 bricks on a wall in a day. How many bricks can 56 ants put on a wall in that time?

$$\begin{array}{r} 56 \\ \times\ 8 \\ \hline 448 \end{array}$$

3. A chorus of grasshoppers sings "Yankee Doodle" 44 times in a day. How many times do they sing in 9 days?

$$\begin{array}{r} 44 \\ \times\ 9 \\ \hline 396 \end{array}$$

4. It takes 76 flies to paint a wall. How many flies does it take to paint 4 walls?

$$\begin{array}{r} 76 \\ \times\ 4 \\ \hline 304 \end{array}$$

5. A hard-working termite can saw 65 boards in a day. How many boards can 7 termites saw?

$$\begin{array}{r} 65 \\ \times\ 7 \\ \hline 455 \end{array}$$

6. Waldo has taught lice to give shampoos. A louse can give 7 shampoos in a day. How many shampoos can it give in 25 days?

$$\begin{array}{r} 25 \\ \times\ 7 \\ \hline 175 \end{array}$$

Page 55

Sam Sillicook's Doughnut Shoppe

Skill: One-Step Multiplication Problems (2-digit factors)

Name _____

Sam Sillicook believes that you should put a little jelly in your belly. He has invented the Super Duper Jelly Doughnuts that are so full of jelly, they leak. His Twisted Circles are drenched in sugar. He has also invented the Banana Cream Doughnut and Jam-Jammed Cream Puffs.

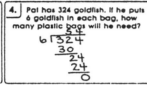

1. Your teacher bought 32 Jam-Jammed Cream Puffs. They cost $.89 each. How much did your teacher spend?

$$\begin{array}{r} .89 \\ \times\ 32 \\ \hline 178 \\ 267 \\ \hline \$28.48 \end{array}$$

2. Harry D. Hulk bought 14 Banana Cream Doughnuts for his breakfast at $.65 each. How much did they cost Harry?

$$\begin{array}{r} .65 \\ \times\ 14 \\ \hline 260 \\ 65 \\ \hline \$9.10 \end{array}$$

3. Your best friend bought 12 Twisted Circles at $.29 each. How much did he spend?

$$\begin{array}{r} .29 \\ \times\ 12 \\ \hline 58 \\ 29 \\ \hline \$3.48 \end{array}$$

4. You love Jam-Jammed Cream Puffs. Your mother buys 17 for your birthday party at $.89 each. How much do they cost?

$$\begin{array}{r} .89 \\ \times\ 17 \\ \hline 623 \\ 89 \\ \hline \$15.13 \end{array}$$

5. Your principal decided to treat the teachers. He bought 24 Super Duper Jelly Doughnuts at $.49 each. What was the total cost?

$$\begin{array}{r} .49 \\ \times\ 24 \\ \hline 196 \\ 98 \\ \hline \$11.76 \end{array}$$

6. Your class was treated to 40 Banana Cream Doughnuts which cost $.65 each. What was the total?

$$\begin{array}{r} .65 \\ \times\ 40 \\ \hline \$26.00 \end{array}$$

Page 56

Buggs I. Lyke

Skill: One-Step Problems with the Four Operations

Name _____

Buggs I. Lyke is in the fast food business. He is the famous inventor of the Beetle Burger which he sells at his store called Beetle in a Box.

1. It takes 300 beetles to make 6 Beetle Burgers. How many beetles are in each Beetle Burger?

$$\frac{50}{6\overline{)300}}$$
30
0

2. Buggs I. Lyke sold 32 orders of Fried Flies on Monday. He sold 6 times as many orders on Saturday. How many orders of Fried Flies were sold on Saturday?

$$\begin{array}{r} 32 \\ \times\ 6 \\ \hline 192 \end{array}$$

3. In July, 342 Cocoon Colas were sold. In August, 298 Cocoon Colas were sold. How many Colas were sold altogether?

$$\begin{array}{r} 342 \\ +298 \\ \hline 640 \end{array}$$

4. There are 35 flies in a regular order of Fried Flies. There are 52 flies in a large order. How many more flies are in a large order?

$$\begin{array}{r} 52 \\ -35 \\ \hline 17 \end{array}$$

5. Buggs uses 69 cocoons to make 3 Cocoon Colas. How many cocoons does it take for one cola?

$$\frac{23}{3\overline{)69}}$$
6
9
9

6. Buggs sold 145 Beetle Burgers on the first day of school. On the next day, he sold 132 Beetle Burgers. How many did he sell in all?

$$\begin{array}{r} 145 \\ +132 \\ \hline 277 \end{array}$$

IF8746 Math Topics

Answer Key

Page 57

Animal Trivia

Name _____

1. A wood rat has a tail which is 23.6 cm long. A deer mouse has a tail 12.2 cm long. What is the difference?

$$23.6 \text{ cm}$$
$$- 12.2 \text{ cm}$$
$$\overline{11.4 \text{ cm}}$$

2. A rock mouse is 26.1 cm long. His tail adds another 14.4 cm. What is his total length from his nose to the tip of his tail?

$$26.1 \text{ cm}$$
$$+ 14.4 \text{ cm}$$
$$\overline{40.5 \text{ cm}}$$

3. A spotted bat has a tail 4.9 cm long. An evening bat has a tail 3.7 cm long. What is the difference?

$$4.9 \text{ cm}$$
$$- 3.7 \text{ cm}$$
$$\overline{1.2 \text{ cm}}$$

4. A pocket gopher has a hind foot 3.5 cm long. A ground squirrel's hind foot is 6.4 cm. How much longer is the ground squirrel's foot?

$$6.4 \text{ cm}$$
$$- 3.5 \text{ cm}$$
$$\overline{2.9 \text{ cm}}$$

5. A cottontail rabbit has ears which are 6.8 cm long. A jackrabbit has ears 12.9 cm long. How much shorter is the cottontail's ear?

$$12.9 \text{ cm}$$
$$- 6.8 \text{ cm}$$
$$\overline{6.1 \text{ cm}}$$

6. A porcupine has a tail 30.0 cm long. A possum has a tail 53.5 cm long. How much longer is the possum's tail?

$$53.5 \text{ cm}$$
$$- 30.0 \text{ cm}$$
$$\overline{23.5 \text{ cm}}$$

7. The hind foot of a river otter is 14.6 cm long. The hind foot of a hog-nosed skunk is 9.0 cm long. What is the difference?

$$14.6 \text{ cm}$$
$$- 9.0 \text{ cm}$$
$$\overline{5.6 \text{ cm}}$$

Page 57

Page 58

The Mystery of the Missing Sweets

Some mysterious person is sneaking away with pieces of desserts from Sam Sillicook's Diner. Help him figure out how much is missing.

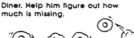

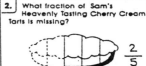

1. What fraction of Sam's Super Sweet Chocolate Cream Cake is missing? $\dfrac{2}{5}$

2. What fraction of Sam's Heavenly Tasting Cherry Cream Tarts is missing? $\dfrac{2}{5}$

3. What fraction of Sam's Tastee Toffee Coffee Cake is missing? $\dfrac{2}{3}$

4. What fraction of Sam's Luscious Licorice Candy Cake is missing?  $\dfrac{7}{12}$

5. What fraction of Sam's Tasty Tidbits of Chocolate Ice Cream is missing? $\dfrac{5}{9}$

6. Sam's Upside-down Ice Cream Cake is very famous. What fraction has vanished? $\dfrac{7}{8}$

Page 58

Page 59

Nat Nit Wit

Name _____

Nat Nit Wit can't tell time. He thinks that a minute is some kind of insect and that a clock is a new kind of soccer ball. He needs your help to solve these problems.

1. Nat is supposed to be at school in 10 minutes. What time should he get there? 9:00

2. Nat started breakfast at 7:10 a.m. It took him 15 minutes to eat. Mark the time he finished. (7:25)

3. Nat will leave school in 5 minutes. What time will it be then? 3:05

4. Nat and his brother Not Nit Wit will eat dinner in 15 minutes. When will that be? 5:00

5. It is now 6:45 p.m. Nat must start his homework in 5 minutes. Mark the starting time on the clock. (6:50)

6. Nat will go to the park in 15 minutes. It is now 1:25 p.m. Mark the time he will go to the park. (1:40)

Page 59

Page 60

Lizzy the Lizard Bags Her Bugs

Name _____

Lizzy the Lizard is a great hunter of insects. She separates her bugs into separate bags so that her lunch is ready for the week. Help her decide how to divide the bugs.

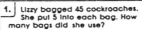
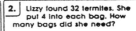

1. Lizzy bagged 45 cockroaches. She put 5 into each bag. How many bags did she use?

$45 \div 5 = 9$

2. Lizzy found 32 termites. She put 4 into each bag. How many bags did she need?

$32 \div 4 = 8$

3. Lizzy captured 49 stinkbugs. She put them into 7 bags. How many stinkbugs were in each bag?

$49 \div 7 = 7$

4. Lizzy captured 27 horn beetles. She used 3 bags. How many beetles went into each bag?

$27 \div 3 = 9$

5. Lizzy lassoed 36 butterflies. She put 9 into each bag. How many bags did she need?

$36 \div 9 = 4$

6. Lizzy went fishing and caught 48 water beetles. She used 6 bags for her catch. How many beetles went into each bag?

$48 \div 6 = 8$

Page 60

Answer Key

"Where's the Bugs?"

Beetle in a Box wants your business. It claims that it uses more bugs in its Beetleburgers, Fried Flies and Cocoon Colas than its competition, McMealworm's. You be the judge by solving these problems.

1. The chef at Beetle in a Box used 180 beetles to make 6 Beetleburgers. How many beetles were used in each burger?

$$6\overline{)180} \quad \begin{array}{r} 30 \\ \underline{18} \\ 0 \end{array}$$

2. The chef at McMealworm's used 203 mealworms to make 7 McMealworm Burgers. How many mealworms were used in each burger?

$$7\overline{)203} \quad \begin{array}{r} 29 \\ 14 \\ 63 \\ 63 \end{array}$$

3. The fry cook at Beetle in a Box used 207 flies to make 9 orders of Fried Flies. How many flies were in each order?

$$9\overline{)207} \quad \begin{array}{r} 23 \\ 18 \\ 27 \\ 27 \end{array}$$

4. The fry cook at McMealworm's used 176 cockroaches to make 8 orders of Roasted Roaches. How many roaches were in each order?

$$8\overline{)176} \quad \begin{array}{r} 22 \\ 16 \\ 16 \\ 16 \end{array}$$

5. It took 140 cocoons to make 7 Cocoon Colas. How many cocoons were used in each Cola?

$$7\overline{)140} \quad \begin{array}{r} 20 \\ 14 \\ 0 \end{array}$$

6. It took 114 crickets to make 6 Cricket Colas. How many crickets were in each Cola?

$$6\overline{)114} \quad \begin{array}{r} 19 \\ 6 \\ 54 \\ 54 \end{array}$$

Page 61

Buggs I. Lyke

Buggs I. Lyke is the world famous owner of such fast food restaurants as Beetle in a Box and McMealworm's. He uses piles of insects in his restaurants. Help him arrange his insects.

1. Buggs uses 30 beetles in his Beetleburger. He has 750 beetles. How many Beetleburgers can he make?

$$30\overline{)750} \quad \begin{array}{r} 25 \\ 60 \\ 150 \\ 150 \end{array}$$

2. Buggs uses 20 mealworms in his Mealburger. How many Mealburgers can he make from 740 mealworms?

$$20\overline{)740} \quad \begin{array}{r} 37 \\ 60 \\ 140 \\ 140 \end{array}$$

3. A Cocoon Cola needs 20 cocoons to get the right flavor. How many Cocoon Colas can he make from 2,440 cocoons?

$$20\overline{)2440} \quad \begin{array}{r} 122 \\ 20 \\ 44 \\ 40 \\ 40 \\ 40 \end{array}$$

4. Buggs needs 30 mealworms for his Jumbo Mealburger. How many Jumbo Mealburgers can he make from 960 mealworms?

$$30\overline{)960} \quad \begin{array}{r} 32 \\ 90 \\ 60 \\ 60 \end{array}$$

5. A large order of Fried Flies uses 60 flies. How many orders of Fried Flies can Buggs make from 3,120 flies?

$$60\overline{)3120} \quad \begin{array}{r} 52 \\ 300 \\ 120 \\ 120 \end{array}$$

6. Buggs makes Moth Shakes. Each shake uses 50 moths. How many shakes can he get from 850 moths?

$$50\overline{)850} \quad \begin{array}{r} 17 \\ 50 \\ 350 \\ 350 \end{array}$$

Page 62

Pat's Pets Aplenty

Pat has just received an enormous shipment of animals to stock his new store, Pat's Pets Aplenty. He needs help separating his animals so that the cats don't end up in the fish tanks and the goldfish don't have to try swimming in the dog cages.

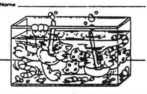

1. Pat received 650 rabbits. He wants to put them in pens of 25 rabbits each. How many rabbit pens does he need?

$$25\overline{)650} \quad \begin{array}{r} 26 \\ 50 \\ 150 \\ 150 \end{array}$$

2. His shipment came with 828 white mice. Pat keeps them in cages of 23 each. How many cages does he need?

$$23\overline{)828} \quad \begin{array}{r} 36 \\ 69 \\ 138 \\ 138 \end{array}$$

3. Pat was sent 1,620 guppies. If he puts 54 guppies in a plastic bag, how many plastic bags will he need?

$$54\overline{)1620} \quad \begin{array}{r} 30 \\ 162 \\ 0 \end{array}$$

4. The delivery truck dropped off 465 puppies. Each puppy pen holds 15 puppies. How many puppy pens does Pat need?

$$15\overline{)465} \quad \begin{array}{r} 31 \\ 45 \\ 15 \\ 15 \end{array}$$

5. Pat was sent 253 king snakes. Each snake tank holds 11 snakes. How many snake tanks does Pat need?

$$11\overline{)253} \quad \begin{array}{r} 23 \\ 22 \\ 33 \\ 33 \end{array}$$

6. Pat received 546 parrots. He keeps them in bird cages with 13 birds in each cage. How many bird cages does Pat need?

$$13\overline{)546} \quad \begin{array}{r} 42 \\ 52 \\ 26 \\ 26 \end{array}$$

Page 63

Smelly Belly Makes Sense, Cents and Scents

Smelly Belly is a skunk with a great fondness for making perfumes. She also likes to make money. She considers this a very sensible thing to do.

1. Smelly Belly's favorite perfume is called Eau de Skunk or Skunk Water. A bottle sells for $7.99. How much will it cost for 3 bottles?

$$\begin{array}{r} \$7.99 \\ \times 3 \\ \hline \$23.97 \end{array}$$

2. Hefty Pig bought a bottle of Eau de Skunk for $7.99 and a bottle of Sweet Stink for $3.78. How much did it cost for both perfumes?

$$\begin{array}{r} \$7.99 \\ +3.78 \\ \hline \$11.77 \end{array}$$

3. Smelly sold a bottle of her cheapest perfume, Polecat, to a rat for $1.99. How much less expensive is Polecat than Sweet Stink?

$$\begin{array}{r} \$3.78 \\ -1.99 \\ \hline \$1.79 \end{array}$$

4. Smelly split 140 bottles of Skunk Musk evenly between her 7 sisters. How many bottles did each sister get?

$$7\overline{)140} \quad \begin{array}{r} 20 \end{array}$$

5. Smelly sold 30 bottles of her Eau de Skunk at $7.99 each. How much money did she get?

$$\begin{array}{r} \$7.99 \\ \times 30 \\ \hline \$239.70 \end{array}$$

6. A bottle of Skunk Cologne for Men costs $7.00 for 7 ounces. How much does each ounce cost?

$$7\overline{)\$7.00} \quad \begin{array}{r} \$1.00 \\ 7 \\ 00 \end{array}$$

Page 64

Answer Key

Percy C. Porcupine: Student for a Day

Skill: One-Step Problems with the Four Operations

Name _____

Percy C. Porcupine loves to learn, so one day he decided to follow his friends to school. He ended up in the 4th grade.

1. Percy spent 55 minutes in math, 65 minutes in reading and 25 minutes in spelling. What was the total time he spent in the classes?

$$\begin{array}{r} 55 \\ 65 \\ +\,25 \\ \hline 145 \end{array}$$

2. Percy loves books. He ate 22 pages from his math book and 10 times as many from his reading book. How many pages did he eat from his reading book?

$$\begin{array}{r} 22 \\ \times\,10 \\ \hline 220 \end{array}$$

3. All 30 children in Percy's class wanted some quills. He split 180 quills evenly among them. How many quills did each child get?

$$30\,\overline{)180}\;\;6 \\ \underline{180}$$

4. Kathy and Ellen decided to pet Percy. Kathy got 131 quills in her hand, and Ellen got 97 quills in her hand. What was the difference?

$$\begin{array}{r} 1\overset{2}{3}1 \\ -\,97 \\ \hline 34 \end{array}$$

5. Percy read 15 words in a minute. At this rate, how many words did he read in 25 minutes?

$$\begin{array}{r} 25 \\ \times\,15 \\ \hline 125 \\ 25 \\ \hline 375 \end{array}$$

6. At morning recess, Percy played tag, and he tagged 16 children Percy. He gave each 27 quills. How many quills did one Percy give out?

$$\begin{array}{r} 16 \\ 27 \\ \hline 432 \end{array}$$

Page 65

Molly Mugwumps

Skill: Two-Step Problems with Addition and Division (Finding the Average)

Name _____

Molly Mugwumps is the best football player but not the best student in the 4th grade. She thinks math and marbles are both something to eat.

1. Molly got a 60%, a 40% and a 20% on 3 spelling tests. What was her average mark? (HINT: Add the scores and divide by 3.)

$$\begin{array}{r} 60\% \\ 40\% \\ +\,20\% \\ \hline 120\% \end{array} \qquad 3\,\overline{)120}\;\;40\% \\ \qquad\qquad \underline{12} \\ \qquad\qquad\quad 0$$

2. Molly rushed for 60 yards in one game, 80 yards in a second game and 70 yards in a third. What was her average number of yards rushing?

$$\begin{array}{r} 60\text{ yd.} \\ 80\text{ yd.} \\ +\,70\text{ yd.} \\ \hline 210\text{ yd.} \end{array} \qquad 3\,\overline{)210}\;\;70\text{ yd} \\ \qquad\qquad \underline{21} \\ \qquad\qquad\quad 0$$

3. Molly took 5 math tests. She got a 35%, a 45%, a 25%, a 50% and a 0%. What was her average mark?

$$\begin{array}{r} 35\% \\ 45\% \\ 25\% \\ 50\% \\ +\,0\% \\ \hline 155\% \end{array} \qquad 5\,\overline{)155}\;\;31\% \\ \qquad\qquad \underline{15} \\ \qquad\qquad\;\; 5 \\ \qquad\qquad\;\; \underline{5} \\ \qquad\qquad\;\; 0$$

4. Molly missed the following number of problems on her math papers: 12, 20, 4, 7 and 2. What was her average number of wrong answers?

$$12+20+4+7+2 = 45$$
$$45 \div 5 = 9$$

5. Molly drank 12 quarts of milk one week, 20 quarts the second week and 28 quarts the third week. What was her weekly average?

$$\begin{array}{r} 12 \\ 20 \\ +\,28 \\ \hline 60 \end{array} \qquad 3\,\overline{)60}\;\;20\text{ qt}. \\ \qquad\quad \underline{6} \\ \qquad\quad 0$$

6. Molly doesn't do very well on tests. She got a 28%, a 34%, a 22% and a 12% on her last 4 social studies tests. What was her average grade?

$$28\% + 34\% + 22\% + 12\% = 96\%$$
$$96\% \div 4 = 24\%$$

Page 66

Shifty Sam's "Super Duper Sale"

Skill: Two-Step Problems with Multiplication and Subtraction

Name _____

Shifty Sam owns a store where you can buy just about anything from sports equipment to the latest fads in clothes and records. But you have to be very careful, or Shifty Sam will cheat you.

1. Shifty Sam sells posters at $.99 each or 3 posters for $2.99 during his sale. Is this a good deal? How much more or less is this than the regular price?

Not a good deal!

$$\begin{array}{r} \$.99 \\ \times\,3 \\ \hline \$2.97 \end{array} \qquad \begin{array}{r} \$2.99 \\ -\,2.97 \\ \hline .02 \end{array} \text{ more at sale price}$$

2. You can buy Spiffle balls that curve and loop for $.67 regularly. Shifty has them on sale now at 5 for $2.99. Do you save money buying them this way? How much?

Yes-a good deal.

$$\begin{array}{r} \$.67 \\ \times\,5 \\ \hline \$3.35 \end{array} \qquad \begin{array}{r} \$3.35 \\ -\,2.99 \\ \hline .36 \end{array} \text{ saved at sale price}$$

3. Sam's Potato Patch Dolls usually sell for $3.99 each. During his sale, they are 2 for $8.99. How much more or less is this than the regular price?

$$\begin{array}{r} \$3.99 \\ \times\,2 \\ \hline \$7.98 \end{array} \qquad \begin{array}{r} \$8.99 \\ -\,7.98 \\ \hline \$1.01 \end{array} \text{ more at sale price}$$

4. The normal price for a package of stickers is $.49. The sale price is 5 for $2.49. Is this a good deal? What is the difference in the cost?

Not a good deal.

$$\begin{array}{r} \$.49 \\ \times\,5 \\ \hline \$2.45 \end{array} \qquad \begin{array}{r} \$2.49 \\ -\,2.45 \\ \hline \$.04 \end{array} \text{ sale price}$$

5. A package of Juicy Spurts Bubble Gum costs $.39. During the sale, Sam is selling 7 packs for $2.39. How much do you save at the sale price?

$$\begin{array}{r} \$.39 \\ \times\,7 \\ \hline \$2.73 \end{array} \qquad \begin{array}{r} \$2.73 \\ -\,2.39 \\ \hline \$.34 \end{array} \text{ less at sale price}$$

6. Sam will sell Iron-On Tee Shirt Designs at $.89 each or 4 for $3.49 during his Super Duper Sale. How much money is saved this way?

$$\begin{array}{r} \$.89 \\ \times\,4 \\ \hline \$3.56 \end{array} \qquad \begin{array}{r} \$3.56 \\ -\,3.49 \\ \hline \$.07 \end{array} \text{ less at sale price}$$

Page 67

Birthday Party at McMealworm's

Skill: Multi-Step Problems with the Four Operations (Mixed)

Name _____

Your mother decides to let you invite your friends to a birthday party at your favorite restaurant, McMealworm's. A McMealworm Burger costs $1.69. A large order of Roasted Roaches costs $.79. A Cricket Cola is $.89.

1. For an appetizer, your mother buys 7 large orders of Roasted Roaches. How much change will she get from a $10.00 bill?

$$\begin{array}{r} \$.79 \\ \times\,7 \\ \hline \$5.53 \end{array} \qquad \begin{array}{r} \$10.00 \\ -\,5.53 \\ \hline \$4.47 \end{array}$$

2. Your friends drink 11 Cricket Colas before dinner. How much will these cost? How much less than $10.00 is this?

$$\begin{array}{r} \$.89 \\ \times\,11 \\ \hline \$9.79 \end{array} \qquad \begin{array}{r} \$10.00 \\ -\,9.79 \\ \hline \$.21 \end{array}$$

3. One of your best friends orders 2 McMealworm Burgers and 3 Cricket Colas. What does it cost for his meal?

$$\begin{array}{r} \$1.69 \\ \times\,2 \\ \hline \$3.38 \end{array} \quad \begin{array}{r} \$.89 \\ \times\,3 \\ \hline \$2.67 \end{array} \quad \begin{array}{r} 3.38 \\ +\,2.67 \\ \hline \$6.05 \end{array}$$

4. Another friend pigs out and buys 6 large orders of Roasted Roaches and 1 McMealworm Burger. What does it cost for that meal?

$$\begin{array}{r} \$.79 \\ \times\,6 \\ \hline \$4.74 \end{array} \quad \begin{array}{r} \$4.74 \\ 1.69 \\ \hline \$6.43 \end{array}$$

5. One of the girls orders 2 McMealworm Burgers and 2 Cricket Colas. What does it cost for her meal?

$$\begin{array}{r} 1.69 \\ \times\,2 \\ \hline \$3.38 \end{array} \quad \begin{array}{r} .89 \\ \times\,2 \\ \hline \$1.78 \end{array} \quad \begin{array}{r} \$3.38 \\ +\,1.78 \\ \hline \$5.16 \end{array}$$

6. The total cost of the party to your mom is exactly $90.00. What is the average cost for your group of 7 boys, 7 girls and 1 parent? (HINT: Find the total number of people and divide.)

$$7 + 7 + 1 = 15$$
$$\$90.00 \div 15 = \$6.00$$

Page 68

Suzy Spider — Interior Decorator

Suzy Spider is decorating her house. She is a very clever decorator, but she needs your help figuring out the area and perimeter.

Name _____

Key Facts:
- Perimeter is the sum of all four sides.
- Area is the length times the width.

1. Suzy is putting a silk fence around her garden. It is 12 cm long and 10 cm wide. What is the perimeter of the garden?

$$12 + 12 + 10 + 10 = 44 cm$$

2. Suzy Spider wants to surround her house with a silk thread. Her house is 17 cm long and 12 cm wide. What is its perimeter?

$$17 + 17 + 12 + 12 = 58 cm$$

3. Suzy wants to carpet her living room. It is 5 cm long and 4 cm wide. How much carpet should she buy for her living room?

$$5 cm \times 4 cm = 20 sq cm$$

4. Suzy put wallpaper on a kitchen wall. The wall is 7 cm tall and 4 cm wide. What is its area?

$$7 cm \times 4 cm = 28 sq cm$$

5. Suzy has decided to hang a silk thread all the way around her porch. The porch is 4 cm long and 3 cm wide. How long should the thread be?

$$4 + 4 + 3 + 3 = 14 cm$$

6. Suzy's bedroom is 6 cm long and 5 cm wide. How much carpet should she buy for it?

$$6 cm \times 5 cm = 30 sq cm$$

Page 69

Krab E. Krabby

Krab E. Krabby carries a yardstick with him everywhere he goes, and he measures everything that he can.

Name _____

Key Facts:
- 12 inches = 1 foot
- 36 inches = 3 feet = 1 yard

1. Krab E. Krabby wanted to measure the length of a grasshopper. Would he use a ruler or a yardstick?

ruler

2. Krab E. Krabby scolded Rollo Rattlesnake because Rollo wouldn't straighten out and cooperate. Should Krab E. Krabby use a ruler or a yardstick to measure Rollo?

yardstick

3. Mr. Krabby measured a garter snake that was 44 inches long. How many yards and inches was this?
___1___ yard __8__ inches left over

$$\begin{array}{r} 44 \text{ in. (yardstick)} \\ -36 \text{ in. (snake)} \\ \hline 8 \text{ in.} \end{array}$$

4. Krab E. measured a tomato hornworm that was 5 inches long. How many inches less than a foot was this?

$$12 in. - 5 in. = 7 in. \text{ less than a foot}$$

5. Mr. Krabby measured a monarch butterfly that was 4 inches wide. How many inches less than a foot was the butterfly?

$$12 in. - 4 in. = 8 in. \text{ less than a foot}$$

6. Krab E. Krabby measured a lazy tuna that was 1 foot 11 inches long. How many total inches was the tuna?

$$\begin{array}{r} 12 \text{ in.} \\ +11 \text{ in.} \\ \hline 23 \text{ in.} \end{array}$$

Page 70

Knowing When to Add – I

Name _____

Learn these key addition words. They will help you know when to add.

more	in all	altogether
total	in addition to	sum

Circle the key addition words and solve the problems.

1. George has 6 railroad cars. Chuck has 8 railroad cars. If they join their railroad cars, how many cars (altogether) will be in their train?

$$6 \oplus 8 = \underline{14}$$

2. Betsy had 5 strings of beads. Her aunt gave her 3 (more). How many strings of beads does she have (altogether)?

$$5 + 3 = 8$$

3. John bought 4 miniature cars. He already had 19. How many miniature cars does John have (in all)?

$$4 + 19 = 23$$

4. Emily has 15 dolls in her collection at home. When the 13 dolls which are in the doll hospital are returned, how many will she have (in all)?

$$15 + 13 = 28$$

5. Molly already had 96 pictures in her album. Then she added 17 (more). How many pictures (in all) does she now have in her album?

$$96 + 17 = 113$$

6. Dean collected 439 baseball cards. Uncle Ben gave him 72 (more). How many baseball cards does Dean have (altogether)?

$$439 + 72 = 511$$

7. Jim had 84 seashells in his collection. He found 25 (more). (Altogether) how many seashells does he have?

$$84 + 25 = 109$$

Page 71

Knowing When to Add – II

Name _____

Circle the key addition words and solve the problems.

1. Jane and her parents rented a lake cottage for two weeks. The first week's rent was $120.00. The second week's rent was $90.00. How much (in all) was the rent for two weeks?

$$\$120.00 \oplus \$90.00 = \$210.00$$

2. Jane bought a swimsuit for $27.00 and fins for $6.00 (in all) how much did her swimming gear cost?

$$\$27.00 + \$6.00 = \$33.00$$

3. The rent on a boat is $8.00 per day, and the rent for a motor is $7.00 per day. How much (altogether) would it cost to rent the boat and motor for a day?

$$\$8.00 + \$7.00 = \$15.00$$

4. It is a 3-mile walk from the cottage to a road on the other side of the lake. It is a 4-mile walk down the road to get to town. How far is it (altogether) to walk from the cottage to town?

$$3 + 4 = 7$$

5. On the first day she was at the lake, Jane caught 7 fish. Her parents caught 12 (more) fish than she did. How many fish did Jane's parents catch?

$$7 + 12 = 19$$

6. Jane bought 65¢ worth of bait (in addition) to the 30¢ worth she already had. How much bait did Jane have (altogether)?

$$65¢ + 30¢ = 95¢$$

7. During the first week Jane spent 28 hours out on the lake. During the second week she was on the lake only 13 hours. How many hours (in all) did Jane spend on the lake?

$$28 + 13 = 41$$

Page 72

Answer Key

Name _____

Knowing When to Add – Review

Circle the key addition words and solve the problems.

1. The choir at Madison School is made up of 26 girls and 18 boys. What is the total choir membership?

$$26 + 18 = 44$$

2. The band at Madison School is composed of 19 girls and 22 boys. How many band members are there in all?

$$19 + 22 = 41$$

3. There are 214 girls and 263 boys attending Madison School. How many students altogether attend Madison School?

$$214 + 263 = 477$$

4. Next fall, in addition to the 477 students already at Madison, 248 more will be bussed in. Altogether, how many students will be at Madison School?

$$477 + 248 = 725$$

5. Mr. Mill's bus route is 14 miles long. Mrs. Albert's route is 17 miles long. Ms. Byrne's route is 15 miles long. How many miles altogether do these 3 bus routes cover?

$$17 + 14 + 15 = 46$$

6. The book rental at Madison is $8.00. The supplies cost $14.00. The locker fee is $3.00. What is the sum of these expenses?

$$\$8.00 + \$14.00 + \$3.00 = \$25.00$$

7. The staff at Madison is made up of 24 teachers, 3 custodians and 2 administrators. How many staff members in all are there?

$$24 + 3 + 2 = 29$$

Page 73

Name _____

Knowing When to Subtract – I

Circle the key subtraction words and solve the problems.

Learn these key subtraction words. They will help you know when to subtract.

fewer
less
left
more

1. Bill and his father planted corn on 120 acres of the farm. They planted wheat on 80 acres. How many fewer acres of wheat did they plant than corn?

$$120 - 80 = 40$$

2. Bill's father sold 16 of his 34 beef cattle. How many cattle were left?

$$34 - 16 = 18$$

3. Bill picked 34 quarts of strawberries. Bill's mother froze 13 of those quarts. How many quarts were left for Bill to sell?

$$34 - 13 = 21$$

4. For his Four-H Club project, Bill is raising 12 hogs. His father has 40 hogs. How many fewer hogs does Bill have than his father?

$$40 - 12 = 28$$

5. Last week Bill's father picked 78 bushels of apples. Bill picked 14 bushels. How many more bushels did his father pick than Bill?

$$78 - 14 = 64$$

6. Bill and his father picked 128 ears of corn and sold 72 of the ears of corn from their roadside stand. How many ears of corn were left?

$$128 - 72 = 56$$

Page 74

Name _____

Knowing When to Subtract – II

Circle the key subtraction words and solve the problems.

1. Jenny and Bob ate lunch at the local burger shop. Jenny paid $1.49 for a cheeseburger. Bob paid $1.25 for a hamburger. How much less did Bob's sandwich cost than Jenny's?

$$\$1.49 - \$1.25 = \$.24$$

2. Jenny had $5.00. She spent $2.49 on her lunch. How much money does she have left?

$$\$5.00 - \$2.49 = \$2.51$$

3. Chilidogs are 99¢ each and hot dogs are 79¢ each. How much less is a hot dog than a chilidog?

$$99¢ - 79¢ = 20¢$$

4. The manager said that yesterday he sold 249 hamburgers and 123 hot dogs. How many more hamburgers were sold than hot dogs?

$$249 - 123 = 126$$

5. Jenny ate a soft ice cream cone which cost 45¢ less than Bob's 95¢ chocolate sundae. How much did the ice cream cone cost?

$$95¢ - 45¢ = 50¢$$

6. This afternoon 27 adults and 15 children were eating in the burger shop. How many more adults were there than children?

$$27 - 15 = 12$$

7. Bill's lunch cost $2.15. Bob's lunch cost $2.60. How much less did Bill pay for his lunch than Bob?

$$\$2.60 - \$2.15 = \$.45$$

Page 75

Name _____

Knowing When to Subtract – Review

Circle the key subtraction words and solve the problems.

1. There are 71 restaurants and 58 grocery stores in Lexington. How many fewer grocery stores than restaurants are there?

$$71 - 58 = 13$$

2. In one part of Lexington 28 of the 113 houses were torn down. How many houses were left standing?

$$113 - 28 = 85$$

3. Lexington has 53 elementary schools and 18 middle schools. How many more elementary schools than middle schools does Lexington have?

$$53 - 18 = 35$$

4. There are 980 doctors and 314 auto mechanics in Lexington. How many more doctors are there than mechanics?

$$980 - 314 = 666$$

5. There are 17 fewer theaters than churches in Lexington. Lexington has 41 churches. How many theaters are there?

$$41 - 17 = 24$$

6. Lexington has 364 miles of two-lane streets and 178 miles of four-lane streets. How many more miles of two-lane streets than four-lane streets does Lexington have?

$$364 - 178 = 186$$

7. Lexington has 12 fewer traffic lights than Knoxville does. Knoxville has 237 traffic lights. How many traffic lights does Lexington have?

$$237 - 12 = 225$$

Page 76

Answer Key

Skill: Discriminating between addition and subtraction problems

Name

Add or Subtract? – Review

Circle the key addition and subtraction words. Then solve the problems.

1. The bakery donated 84 doughnuts for the sunrise breakfast. Of the 84 doughnuts, 65 were eaten. How many doughnuts were left uneaten?

$$84 - 65 = 19$$

2. The baker baked 204 cookies. He added chocolate chips to 96 of them. How many cookies were left without chocolate chips?

$$204 - 96 = 108$$

3. Tom ate 12 cookies. Bill ate 13 cookies. Ann ate 11 cookies. What was the total number of cookies eaten?

$$12 + 13 + 11 = 36$$

4. The baker baked 37 apple pies and 44 pumpkin pies. How many more pumpkin pies than apple pies did he bake?

$$44 - 37 = 7$$

5. The baker iced 172 doughnuts and dipped 137 fewer doughnuts in powdered sugar. How many doughnuts were dipped in powdered sugar?

$$172 - 137 = 35$$

6. In one week the baker sold 192 layer cakes in addition to 265 sheet cakes. How many cakes did he sell altogether?

$$192 + 265 = 457$$

7. Yesterday the baker sold 72 peach pies, 49 banana cream pies and 12 sugar cream pies. That is a total of how many pies?

$$72 + 49 + 12 = 133$$

Page 77

Skill: Introducing multiplication clues

Name

Knowing When to Multiply — I

Learn these key words. They will help you know when to multiply.

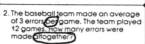

| times | each | per | in all | altogether |

Circle the key multiplication words and solve the problems.

1. There are 6 baseball teams in the city league. Each team has 9 players. How many players in all are there in the city league?

$$6 \otimes 9 = 54$$

2. The baseball team made an average of 3 errors per game. The team played 12 games. How many errors were made altogether?

$$3 \times 12 = 36$$

3. The basketball team averaged 62 points per game. The team played 20 games this season. How many points did the team score in all?

$$62 \times 20 = 1,240$$

4. A baseball glove costs $38.00. How much altogether would it cost to buy 9 gloves?

$$\$38.00 \times 9 = \$342.00$$

5. Each player's uniform costs $53.00. In all, how much would it cost to outfit 9 players?

$$\$53.00 \times 9 = \$477.00$$

6. Jeff swam 35 laps in the pool each day for 30 days. How many laps did he swim altogether?

$$35 \times 30 = 1,050$$

7. Swim trunks cost $4.00 each. It costs 65 times that much to outfit a football player. How much would it cost to outfit a football player?

$$\$4.00 \times 65 = \$260.00$$

Page 78

Name

Knowing When to Multiply — II

Circle the key multiplication words and solve the problems.

Learn these key words. They will help you know when to multiply.

per
times
each
altogether
in all

1. Emily works in her father's fruit and vegetable stand on weekends. She worked 8 hours each Saturday for 4 weeks. How many hours altogether did Emily work during those 4 weeks?

$$8 \times 4 = 32$$

2. Apples sell for 30¢ each. How much would 3 apples cost?

$$30¢ \times 3 = 90¢$$

3. Emily found that each orange weighs 8 ounces. How much in all would 12 oranges weigh?

$$8 \times 12 = 96$$

4. A large bag of grapefruit sells for 2 times the price of a bag of onions. The bag of onions sells for $1.30. What is the price of the large bag of grapefruit?

$$2 \times \$1.30 = \$2.60$$

5. Mr. Long bought a bunch of bananas which weighed 3 pounds. Bananas sell for 32¢ per pound. How much in all did the bananas cost?

$$3 \times 32¢ = 96¢$$

6. Grocery bags cost 3¢ each. During one morning Emily used 27 different bags. Altogether how much did the bags cost?

$$3¢ \times 27 = 81¢$$

Page 79

Name

Knowing When to Multiply — III

Circle the key multiplication words and solve the problems.

1. Jack cuts and sells firewood. He cuts 6 cords of firewood per day. How many cords does he cut in 5 days?

$$6 \times 5 = 30$$

2. Firewood sells for $32.00 per cord. How much money does Jack receive in all for 6 cords.?

$$\$32.00 \times 6 = \$192.00$$

3. Jack sold $128.00 worth of firewood to one customer and 7 times that amount to a store owner. How much did the store owner pay Jack?

$$\$128.00 \times 7 = \$896.00$$

4. If Jack cuts and sells 30 cords of wood, how much would Jack receive altogether at $32.00 per cord?

$$30 \times \$32.00 = \$960.00$$

5. Chain saw blades sell for $6.50 each. Jack buys 5 each week. How much in all does Jack spend for chain saw blades during one week?

$$\$6.50 \times 5 = \$32.50$$

6. Each day Jack uses 4 gallons of gasoline in his chain saw. How many gallons altogether does Jack use in 5 days?

$$4 \times 5 = 20$$

7. Gasoline costs Jack $3.68 per day. In all, what is his cost for gasoline for 5 days?

$$\$3.68 \times 5 = \$18.40$$

Page 80

Answer Key

Page 81

Multiply or Add?

Circle the key multiplication and addition words and solve the problems.

1. The Davis family went on a 7-day trip. They averaged 420 miles per day. How many miles in all did they travel?

$$7 \times 420 = 2,940$$

2. The Davis family usually drove 55 miles per hour. How many miles in all could they cover in 6 hours at this speed?

$$55 \times 6 = 330$$

3. On the second day of the trip Mr. Davis ran over some glass and had to replace 2 tires. The cost was $80.00 per tire. Altogether how much did the tire replacement cost?

$$2 \times \$80.00 = \$160.00$$

4. On the second day they traveled only 170 miles. On the third they covered 540 miles. How many miles altogether did they travel during those days?

$$170 + 540 = 710$$

5. The Davis family ate in 3 different restaurants on each of the 7 days. Altogether, in how many different restaurants did they eat?

$$3 \times 7 = 21$$

6. During the first 3 days of the trip, the Davis family traveled through 34 towns. During the last 4 days they went through 37 towns. How many towns did they travel through in all?

$$34 + 37 = 71$$

7. On the last day of the trip, the Davis family left for home at 6:00 A.M. and arrived 9 hours later. They drove at the average rate of 50 miles per hour. How far did they travel in all on the last day?

$$9 \times 50 = 450$$

Page 81

Page 82

Multiply or Subtract?

Circle the key multiplication and subtraction words and solve the problems.

1. Bill works 3 hours per day in a tire store. How many hours altogether does Bill work in 5 days?

$$3 \times 5 = 15$$

2. There are 94 auto tires and 37 truck tires in the store. How many fewer truck tires are there than auto tires?

$$94 - 37 = 57$$

3. The store had 94 auto tires in stock. One day Bill sold 16 auto tires. How many of the 94 auto tires were left?

$$94 - 16 = 78$$

4. The manager told Bill to order 3 times as many auto tires as truck tires. Bill ordered 18 truck tires. How many auto tires should he order?

$$3 \times 18 = 54$$

5. Each truck tire weighs 80 pounds. How much altogether do 6 truck tires weigh?

$$80 \times 6 = 480$$

6. A truck tire weighs 80 pounds. An auto tire weighs 18 pounds. How many more pounds does a truck tire weigh than an auto tire?

$$80 - 18 = 62$$

7. The 4 tires for a Ford car cost $184.00. The 4 tires for a Dodge car cost $240.00. How much less do the tires cost for the Ford than the Dodge?

$$240.00 - 184.00 = \$56.00$$

Page 82

Page 83

Knowing When to Divide – I

Learn these key words. They will help you know when to divide.

each   per

Circle the key division words and solve the problems.

1. While at the grocery store with her mother, Doris spent 36¢ for pencils. The pencils cost 6¢ each. How many pencils did she buy?

$$36¢ \div 6¢ = 6¢$$

2. Doris's mother bought 2 bags of apples for $2.40. How much did she pay per bag?

$$\$2.40 \div 2 = \$1.20$$

3. The 2 bags of apples together contained 16 apples. How many apples were in each bag?

$$16 \div 2 = 8$$

4. The grocer sold 3 oranges for 39¢. That is how much per orange?

$$39¢ \div 3 = 13¢$$

5. Doris bought 4 rolls of mints for 96¢. How much did she pay for each roll?

$$96¢ \div 4 = 24¢$$

6. Doris bought a package of 30 cookies. If the cookies were divided evenly between the 5 members of Doris's family, how many cookies would each person get?

$$30 \div 5 = 6$$

7. Doris's mother bought 4 pounds of meat which cost her $8.80. What was the price per pound?

$$\$8.80 \div 4 = \$2.20$$

Page 83

Page 84

Knowing When to Divide — II

Circle the key division words and solve the problems.

Learn these key words. They will help you know when to divide.

each   per

1. The track team had 28 athletes trying out for 4 open positions. That is an average of how many athletes per position?

$$28 \div 4 = 7$$

2. The girls' and the boys' basketball teams have the same record of wins. Together they won a total of 28 games. That is how many wins per team?

$$28 \div 2 = 14$$

3. In a recent game 6 basketball players scored 42 points. How many points is that per player?

$$42 \div 6 = 7$$

4. The baseball team played 8 games away from home. The team traveled a total of 96 miles. That is an average of how many miles per trip?

$$96 \div 8 = 12$$

5. 92 practice suits were issued to those students trying out for 4 different athletic teams. If the same number of suits were issued for each sport, how many students were out for each sport?

$$92 \div 4 = 23$$

6. During 5 days of practice the basketball team used 75 towels. How many towels were used per day?

$$75 \div 5 = 15$$

Page 84

©1992 Instructional Fair, Inc.

IF8746 Math Topics

Answer Key

Skill: Using division clues

Name _____

Knowing When to Divide — III

Circle the key division words and solve the problems.

1. The 7 members of Dan's scout troop earned $56.00 for new equipment. How much per scout was earned?

$$\$56.00 \div 7 = \$8.00$$

2. On the scouts' camping trip Dan took 24 pictures. How many rolls of film did Dan use if each roll takes 8 pictures?

$$24 \div 8 = 3$$

3. On the camping trip the 7 scouts ate 42 hot dogs. How many hot dogs per scout were eaten?

$$42 \div 7 = 6$$

4. At breakfast 21 eggs were eaten by the 7 scouts. How many eggs were eaten per scout?

$$21 \div 7 = 3$$

5. Later 5 of the scouts caught a total of 35 fish. How many fish did each scout catch?

$$35 \div 5 = 7$$

6. The troop took a 4-hour hike and covered 16 miles. How many miles per hour did the troop cover?

$$16 \div 4 = 4$$

7. During the morning exercises the 7 scouts did a total of 168 sit-ups. How many sit-ups per scout were done?

$$168 \div 7 = 24$$

Skill: Using division clues

Name _____

Knowing When to Divide — IV

Circle the key division words and solve the problems.

1. Susan worked 9 arithmetic problems in 54 minutes. How many minutes did she use for each problem?

$$54 \div 9 = 6$$

2. Jeff worked 9 problems in 63 minutes. He used how many minutes per problem?

$$63 \div 9 = 7$$

3. On an achievement test the class was allowed 27 minutes to work 9 problems. How many minutes were allowed for each problem?

$$27 \div 9 = 3$$

4. On a recent test the teacher found that the class made 72 errors. That was an average of 3 errors per student. How many students are in the class?

$$72 \div 3 = 24$$

5. The 5-member mathematics team won 35 ribbons this semester. How many ribbons per member were won?

$$35 \div 5 = 7$$

6. The 5-member team winning the state math contest received $10,000 in scholarships. How much scholarship money did each member win?

$$\$10,000.00 \div 5 = \$2,000.00$$

7. The runner-up team in the state math contest received $7,500 in scholarships. How much scholarship money was awarded each of the 5 members?

$$\$7,500.00 \div 5 = \$1,500.00$$

Name _____

Add or Divide?

Circle the key addition and division words. Then solve the problems.

1. Pam read 32 books in 8 weeks. How many books did she read per week?

$$32 \div 8 = \underline{4}$$

2. Peter read 30 books in 6 weeks. How many books per week did Peter read?

$$30 \div 6 = 5$$

3. The 14 girls in Pam's class read a total of 56 books. The 13 boys read a total of 39 books. How many books in all were read by Pam's classmates?

$$56 + 39 = 95$$

4. The library in Pam's school contains 96 books which Pam would like to read. If Pam reads 4 books each week, how many weeks will it take her to read them all?

$$96 \div 4 = 24$$

5. Pam has 28 books in her own library. She was given 4 more books for her birthday. How many books in all does Pam now have?

$$28 + 4 = 32$$

6. Pam read 84 pages on Saturday, 51 pages on Sunday and 17 pages on Monday. How many pages in all did Pam read?

$$84 + 51 + 17 = 152$$

7. Pam bought 2 new books. One cost $4.50 and the other cost $3.50. How much altogether did Pam pay for the 2 books?

$$\$4.50 + \$3.50 = \$8.00$$

Name _____

Subtract or Divide?

Circle the key subtraction and division words. Then solve the problems.

1. The bus took 44 students to the Kennedy Space Center. Of the students, 19 were girls and 25 were boys. How many more boys were there than girls?

$$25 - 19 = \underline{6}$$

2. While in space an astronaut has 34 different food choices. Jan has 7 food choices at home. How many fewer food choices does Jan have than an astronaut?

$$34 - 7 = 27$$

3. The equipment aboard the satellite will operate for 402 days. After one year (365 days) has passed, how many more days will the equipment work?

$$402 - 365 = 37$$

4. A 7-day week on Pluto would be 980 Earth hours long. How many hours are in each Pluto day?

$$980 \div 7 = 140$$

5. A day on Mercury is 2,100 Earth hours long. A Venus day is 5,400 hours long. A day on Mercury is how many Earth hours fewer than a day on Venus?

$$5,400 - 2,100 = 3,300$$

6. Voyager came within 240,000 miles of Jupiter. That distance would be how many more miles than the 3,000 miles it takes to travel from New York to Seattle?

$$240,000 - 3,000 = 237,000$$

7. It takes the planet Uranus 84 years to revolve around the Sun. During that time Jupiter revolves around the Sun 7 times. How many years does each of Jupiter's revolutions take?

$$84 \div 7 = 12$$

     IF8746 Math Topics

Answer Key

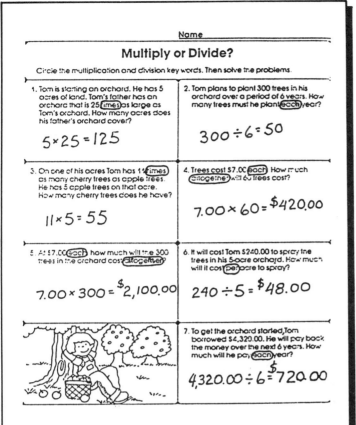

Name

Multiply or Divide?

Circle the multiplication and division key words. Then solve the problems.

1. Tom is starting an orchard. He has 5 acres of land. Tom's father has an orchard that is 25 (times) as large as Tom's orchard. How many acres does his father's orchard cover?

$5 \times 25 = 125$

2. Tom plans to plant 300 trees in his orchard over a period of 6 years. How many trees must he plant (each) year?

$300 \div 6 = 50$

3. On one of his acres Tom has 11 (times) as many cherry trees as apple trees. He has 5 apple trees on that acre. How many cherry trees does he have?

$11 \times 5 = 55$

4. Trees cost $7.00 (each). How much (altogether) will 60 trees cost?

$7.00 \times 60 = \$420.00$

5. At $7.00 (each) how much will the 300 trees in the orchard cost (altogether)?

$7.00 \times 300 = \$2,100.00$

6. It will cost Tom $240.00 to spray the trees in his 5-acre orchard. How much will it cost (per) acre to spray?

$240 \div 5 = \$48.00$

7. To get the orchard started, Tom borrowed $4,320.00. He will pay back the money over the next 6 years. How much will he pay (each) year?

$4,320.00 \div 6 = \$720.00$

Page 89

Skill: Review of problem solving skills

Name

Review Problems

Circle the key words and solve the problems.

1. The 24 third grade students at Dogwood School, along with the 209 other Dogwood students, took part in the annual clean-up day. (Altogether) how many students from Dogwood helped with the clean-up?

$24 + 209 = 233$

2. Students from 8 different rooms at Dogwood School collected a (total of) 128 bags of trash. How many bags (per) room is that?

$128 \div 8 = 16$

3. The fourth grade students collected 4 bags (fewer) than the 17 bags the third grade students collected. How many bags of trash were collected by the fourth grade students?

$17 - 4 = 13$

4. While collecting trash, the Dogwood students also collected 28 pounds of aluminum cans. At 3¢ (per) pound, how much were the aluminum cans worth?

$28 \times 3¢ = 84¢$

5. Dogwood students collected 128 bags of trash. This was 38 bags (more) than the Hickory Hills students collected. How many bags of trash did the Hickory Hills students collect?

$128 - 38 = 90$

6. Pickup trucks hauled the bags of trash away. One truck hauled 56 bags, and the other hauled 47 bags away. How many bags of trash were hauled (altogether) by the two trucks?

$56 + 47 = 103$

7. The newspaper published the winning essay "Keeping Our Community Clean." Of the 209 Dogwood students, 87 entered the contest. That left how many Dogwood students who did not enter the essay contest?

$209 - 87 = 122$

Page 90

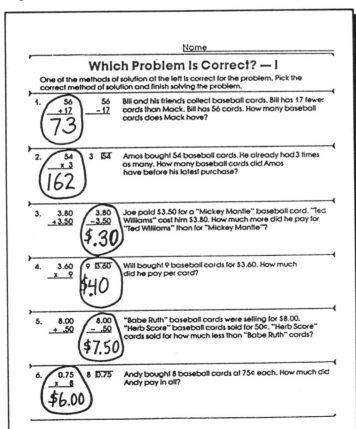

Name

Which Problem Is Correct? — I

One of the methods of solution at the left is correct for the problem. Pick the correct method of solution and finish solving the problem.

1.
$$\begin{array}{r} 56 \\ +17 \\ \hline \mathbf{73} \end{array} \qquad \begin{array}{r} 56 \\ -17 \end{array}$$
Bill and his friends collect baseball cards. Bill has 17 fewer cards than Mack. Bill has 56 cards. How many baseball cards does Mack have?

2.
$$\begin{array}{r} 54 \\ \times 3 \\ \hline \mathbf{162} \end{array} \qquad 3 \overline{\smash{)}54}$$
Amos bought 54 baseball cards. He already had 3 times as many. How many baseball cards did Amos have before his latest purchase?

3.
$$\begin{array}{r} 3.80 \\ +3.50 \end{array} \qquad \begin{array}{r} 3.80 \\ -3.50 \\ \hline \mathbf{\$.30} \end{array}$$
Joe paid $3.50 for a "Mickey Mantle" baseball card. "Ted Williams" cost him $3.80. How much more did he pay for "Ted Williams" than for "Mickey Mantle"?

4.
$$\begin{array}{r} 3.60 \\ \times 9 \end{array} \qquad 9 \overline{\smash{)}3.60}$$
$$\mathbf{\$.40}$$
Will bought 9 baseball cards for $3.60. How much did he pay per card?

5.
$$\begin{array}{r} 8.00 \\ +\ .50 \end{array} \qquad \begin{array}{r} 8.00 \\ -\ .50 \\ \hline \mathbf{\$7.50} \end{array}$$
"Babe Ruth" baseball cards were selling for $8.00. "Herb Score" baseball cards sold for 50¢. "Herb Score" cards sold for how much less than "Babe Ruth" cards?

6.
$$\begin{array}{r} 0.75 \\ \times\ 8 \end{array} \qquad 8 \overline{\smash{)}0.75}$$
$$\mathbf{\$6.00}$$
Andy bought 8 baseball cards at 75¢ each. How much did Andy pay in all?

Page 91

Name

Which Problem Is Correct? — II

The solution at the left is correct for one of the problems to the right. Draw a line under the problem that goes with the solution. Then compute the answer.

1.
$$\begin{array}{r} 6744 \\ -698 \\ \hline \mathbf{6,046} \end{array}$$
a) The local zoo has an elephant which weighs 6,744 pounds. The bear weighs 698 pounds. The bear weighs how much less than the elephant?

b) An elephant at the zoo weighs 6,744 pounds. The bear weighs 698 pounds. Together, how much do they weigh?

2.
$$\begin{array}{r} 12 \\ \times 6 \\ \hline \mathbf{72} \end{array}$$
a) Each of the 6 lions at the zoo gets 12 pounds of meat to eat each day. How much meat is needed to feed the lions for one day?

b) 12 pounds of meat is shared each day by the 6 lions at the zoo. How much meat does each lion get?

3.
$$\begin{array}{r} 213 \\ +78 \\ \hline \mathbf{291} \end{array}$$
a) The zoo had 213 animals and gave 78 to another city that was starting a zoo. How many animals were left?

b) The zoo had 213 animals and was given 78 more. How many animals in all does the zoo have?

4.
$$4 \overline{\smash{)}36}$$
$$\mathbf{9}$$
a) The zoo has 4 times as many monkeys as zebras. There are 36 monkeys. How many zebras are there?

b) The zoo has 4 times as many zebras as monkeys. There are 36 monkeys. How many zebras are there?

5.
$$\begin{array}{r} 350 \\ \times 7 \\ \hline \mathbf{2450} \end{array}$$
a) Last week the attendance at the zoo was 350. How many people went to the zoo on each of the 7 days?

b) Last week the attendance at the zoo averaged 350 people per day. How many people went to the zoo during those 7 days?

6.
$$\begin{array}{r} 248 \\ \times 2 \\ \hline \mathbf{496} \end{array}$$
a) Because of financial problems, the zoo must double attendance or double the ticket price. The average daily attendance is 248. What must attendance be so that the ticket price remains the same?

b) The average daily attendance at the zoo is 248. This is twice the number needed to meet costs. How many tickets must be sold to meet costs?

Page 92

Answer Key

Which Problem Is Correct? — III

The solution at the left is correct for one of the problems to the right. Draw a line under the correct problem. Then compute the answer.

1. 16×8 **128**
   a) It is 8 times as far to Detroit as it is to Grandmother's house. It is 16 miles to Grandmother's house. How far is it to Detroit?
   b) It is 8 times as far to Grandmother's house as to Detroit. It is 16 miles to Grandmother's house. How far is it to Detroit?

2. $2\overline{)1150}$ **575**
   a) It is twice as far from Detroit to Des Moines as from Detroit to Dallas. It is 1,150 miles from Detroit to Dallas. How far is it from Detroit to Des Moines?
   b) It is twice as far from Detroit to Dallas as it is from Detroit to Des Moines. It is 1,150 miles from Detroit to Dallas. How far is it from Detroit to Des Moines?

3. $8.15 - 6.75$ **1.40**
   a) A bus ticket to Frankenmuth costs $8.15. A ticket to Detroit costs $6.75. How much do the 2 tickets cost altogether?
   b) A bus ticket to Frankenmuth costs $8.15. A ticket to Detroit costs $6.75. How much more does it cost to go to Frankenmuth than to Detroit?

4. 150×8 **1200**
   a) It is 150 miles round trip from Bob's home to the University of Michigan. In his freshman year Bob made the trip 8 times. How many miles altogether did he travel?
   b) Bob made 8 trips to the University of Michigan. He traveled a total of 1,200 miles. How far did he travel on each trip?

5. $3\overline{)552}$ **184**
   a) On vacation this year the Adams family traveled 552 miles. Last year they traveled 3 times as far. How many miles did they travel last year?
   b) On vacation last year the Adams family traveled 3 times as far as they did this year. Last year they traveled 552 miles. How far did they travel this year?

6. 595×5 **2975**
   a) The Willis family traveled across the U.S. in 5 days. They averaged 595 miles per day. How far did they travel in all?
   b) The Willis family traveled 595 miles in 5 days. How far did they travel each day?

Page 93

Too Much Information — I

Each problem on this page contains a fact which is not needed in the solution. This unused fact is called a distractor. Underline the distractor in each problem. Then solve the problem.

1. Wild bird seed costs 23¢ per pound. The birds eat 81 pounds of wild bird seed each week. How many pounds of wild bird seed is needed for 52 weeks?
   $81 \times 52 = 4,212$

2. Wild bird seed costs 23¢ per pound. The birds eat 8 pounds of wild bird seed each week. How long will 200 pounds last?
   $200 \div 8 = 25$

3. One day 25 cardinals, 18 gold finches and 19 purple finches ate at the feeders. How many finches were fed?
   $18 + 19 = 37$

4. One afternoon 26 titmice, 14 nuthatches and 17 downy woodpeckers visited the feeders. How many more titmice were there than nuthatches?
   $26 - 14 = 12$

5. One morning 83 birds ate sunflower seeds, 27 birds ate wild bird seed and 19 birds ate earthworms. How many birds ate seed?
   $83 + 27 = 110$

6. One morning 17 cardinals ate at the feeder containing sunflower seed. 14 robins and 12 towhees ate worms from the ground. Mr. Phillips figured each sunflower seed eater ate 3¢ worth. How much did the birds' sunflower seed feast cost Mr. Phillips?
   $17 \times 3¢ = 51¢$

7. Mr. Phillips spent a total of $180.00 for sunflower seed and wild bird seed. The average cost was 30¢ per pound. He spent $34.50 on 150 pounds of wild bird seed. How much did he spend for 450 pounds of sunflower seed?
   $\$180.00 - \$34.50 = \$145.50$

Page 94

Too Much Information — II

Underline the distractor and solve the problems.

1. All 20 of the students from Sandy's class went to the movies. Tickets cost $1.50 each. Drinks cost 55¢ each. How much altogether did the students spend on tickets?
   $20 \times \$1.50 = \$30.00$

2. Of the students, 11 were girls and 9 were boys. At $1.50 per ticket, how much did the boys' tickets cost altogether?
   $9 \times \$1.50 = \$13.50$

3. While 5 students had ice cream, 12 others had candy. Ice cream cost 75¢ per cup. How much did the students spend on ice cream?
   $5 \times \$.75 = \$3.75$

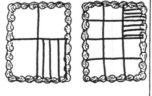

4. 7 of the 20 students did not like the movie. 3 of the 20 students had seen the movie before. How many students had not seen the movie before?
   $20 - 3 = 17$

5. Mary paid 55¢ for an orange drink and 65¢ for a candy bar. Sarah paid 45¢ for popcorn. How much did Mary's refreshments cost her?
   $\$.55 + .65 = \$1.20$

6. 6 of the students spent a total of $16.50 for refreshments and $9.00 for their tickets. How much did each spend for refreshments?
   $\$16.50 \div 6 = \$2.75$

7. 10 of the students went back to see the movie again the next day. Each student paid $1.50 for a ticket, 45¢ for popcorn and 55¢ for a soft drink. How much did each student pay?
   $\$1.50 + .45 + .55 = \$2.50$

Page 95

Picture the Problem — I

Draw a picture of each problem. Then solve the problem.

1. Charley cut his pizza in 3rds and gave one piece to Sherry. George cut his pizza in 6ths and gave Sherry 3 pieces. Which boy gave Sherry the most pizza?

Charley   George
George

2. Harold cut a cherry pie into 6ths and a peach pie into 9ths. He ate 2 pieces of cherry pie and 2 pieces of peach pie. Which pie did he eat the most of?

Cherry   Peach
Cherry

3. Sally cut her cake into 12ths. Sally ate 2 of the 12ths. Joe ate 1/4 of the cake. Who ate the most cake?

Joe   Sally
Joe

4. Betsy and Emily each bought a foot-long hot dog. Betsy divided her hot dog into 6 equal parts and gave Sam 1 of the 6ths. Emily divided her hot dog into 12 equal parts and gave Sam 2 of the 12ths. Who gave Sam the most hot dog?

Betsy   Emily
They each gave him the same amount.

Page 96

Page 97

Name

Picture the Problem — II

Draw a picture of each problem. Then solve the problem.

1. Andy had two ropes of the same length. He cut one rope into 2 equal parts and gave the 2 halves to Bill. The other rope he cut into 4ths and gave 2 of the 4ths to Sue. Who got the most rope?

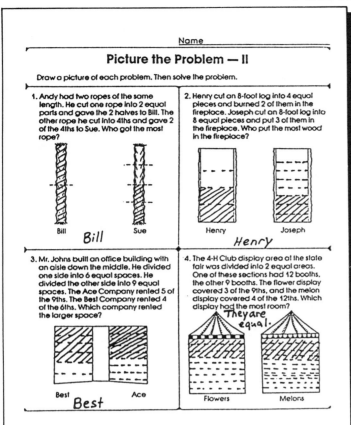

Bill

Sue

Bill

2. Henry cut an 8-foot log into 4 equal pieces and burned 2 of them in the fireplace. Joseph cut an 8-foot log into 8 equal pieces and put 3 of them in the fireplace. Who put the most wood in the fireplace?

Henry   Joseph

Henry

3. Mr. Johns built an office building with an aisle down the middle. He divided one side into 6 equal spaces. He divided the other side into 9 equal spaces. The Ace Company rented 5 of the 9ths. The Best Company rented 4 of the 6ths. Which company rented the larger space?

Best   Ace

Best

4. The 4-H Club display area of the state fair was divided into 2 equal areas. One of these sections had 12 booths, the other 9 booths. The flower display covered 3 of the 9ths, and the melon display covered 4 of the 12ths. Which display had the most room?

They are equal.

Flowers   Melons

Page 98

Name

Time Problems — I

Draw the hands on the clocks to show the starting time and the ending time. Then write the answer to the problem.

1. Molly left school at 3:30 p.m. It took her 20 minutes to walk home. What time did she get home?

Answer: **3:50 p.m.**

2. John's ball game started at 4:05 p.m. and lasted for 2 hours and 30 minutes. What time did the game end?

Answer: **6:35 p.m.**

3. Ann and Beth arrived at the ice cream store at 2:15 p.m. and left for home 40 minutes later. What time did they leave the ice cream store?

Answer: **2:55 p.m.**

4. The school day starts at 8:00 a.m. and ends 6 hours and 45 minutes later. What time does school end?

Answer: **2:45 p.m.**

5. Don's sister Beth was on the phone from 3:45 p.m. until 4:15 p.m. How long was Beth on the phone?

Answer: **30 minutes**

6. Joyce started her bath at 8:35 p.m. and got out at 9:15 p.m. How long was Joyce in the bathtub?

Answer: **40 minutes**

Page 99

Name

Time Problems — II

Draw the hands on the clocks to show the starting time and the ending time. Then write the answer to the problem.

1. The bike race started at 2:55 p.m. and lasted 2 hours and 10 minutes. What time did the race end?

Answer: **5:05 p.m.**

2. Sherry walked in the 12 mile Hunger Walk. She started at 12:30 p.m. and finished at 4:50 p.m. How long did she walk?

Answer: **4 hrs. 20 min.**

3. The 500 mile auto race started at 11:00 a.m. and lasted 2 hours and 25 minutes. What time did the race end?

Answer: **1:25 p.m.**

4. The train left Indianapolis at 7:25 a.m. and arrived in Chicago at 10:50 a.m. How long did the trip take?

Answer: **3 hrs. 25 min.**

5. The chili cook-off started at 10:00 a.m. and all the chili was cooked by 4:30 p.m. How long did it take to cook the chili?

Answer: **6 hrs. 30 min.**

6. The chili judging began at 4:30 p.m. After 3 hours and 45 minutes the chili had all been eaten. At what time was the chili eating finished?

Answer: **8:15 p.m.**

Page 100

Name

Planning Your Attack

Write your method of solution for each of the following problems. The first one is done for you.

1. If you know the price of a circus ticket and you pay for it with a ten dollar bill, how do you figure the amount of change you will get?

Subtract the price of the ticket from $10.00

2. If you know the price of a circus ticket, how do you find the total cost of tickets for you and 2 of your friends?

Multiply the price of the ticket by 3.

3. If you know how many clowns are now performing and how many are yet to appear, how do you find the number of clowns in the circus?

Add the number now performing to the number yet to appear.

4. You know the total number of shows the circus performs in a year and the number they have already performed. How do you find the number left to be performed this year?

Subtract the number already performed from the total number of shows.

5. If you know the amount you paid for 3 bags of popcorn, how do you find the cost of one bag?

Divide the total cost of popcorn by 3.

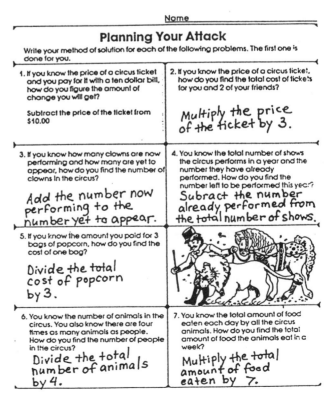

6. You know the number of animals in the circus. You also know there are four times as many animals as people. How do you find the number of people in the circus?

Divide the total number of animals by 4.

7. You know the number of food eaten each day by all the circus animals. How do you find the total amount of food the animals eat in a week?

Multiply the total amount of food eaten by 7.

Answer Key

Page 101

Name

Problem Solving Review — I

Solve the following problems.

1. You weigh 145 pounds and your space suit weighs 250 pounds. How much would you weigh in all when you climb into your spaceship?

$$145 + 250 = 395$$

2. Apollo 10 traveled at a speed which was 450 times the speed of a car traveling down the highway at 55 miles per hour. What was the speed of Apollo 10?

$$450 \times 55 = 24{,}750$$

3. John Glenn spent a little less than 5 hours in space. Sally Ride spent 14 days and 8 hours in space. How many hours did Sally Ride spend in space?

$$(24 \times 14) + 8 = 344$$

4. During 2 flights, Owen Garriott spent 69 days in space. Garriott spent 3 times as long in space as did Eugene Cernan. How many days did Cernan spend in space?

$$69 \div 3 = 23$$

5. The space shuttle at liftoff weighs about 4,500,000 pounds. How much heavier than the earth vehicle you travel in, which weighs around 2,000 pounds?

$$4{,}500{,}000 - 2{,}000 = 4{,}498{,}000$$

6. A space orbiter is as tall as a 12-story building. If each of the 12 stories is 14 feet tall, how tall is the orbiter?

$$12 \times 14 = 168$$

7. When the work is done in space and the shuttle re-enters Earth's atmosphere, it gets very hot. The temperature on the nose of the shuttle gets up to 30 times as hot as the temperature here on a 90°F day. How hot is the nose of the shuttle?

$$90 \times 30 = 2{,}700$$

Page 102

Name

Problem Solving Review — II

Solve the following problems.

1. On a clear night you can see about 2,700 stars. In one year you can see some 6,000 different stars. How many more stars would you see in one year than in one night?

$$6{,}000 - 2{,}700 = 3{,}300$$

2. The exosphere begins at about 250 miles above the Earth and stretches to about 800 miles above Earth. How deep is the exosphere?

$$800 - 250 = 550$$

3. The distance from the sun to Earth, called one astronomical unit (AU), is 93 million miles. The distance from the sun to Jupiter is 5 AU's. How many miles is it from the sun to Jupiter?

$$93{,}000{,}000 \times 5 = 465{,}000{,}000$$

4. Neptune is 30 AU's from the sun. An AU is 93 million miles. How many miles is Neptune from the sun?

$$93{,}000{,}000 \times 30 = 2{,}790{,}000{,}000$$

5. It is about 3,000 miles across the U.S. It is 80 times that distance from Earth to the Earth's moon. How far is it from Earth to the Earth's moon?

$$3{,}000 \times 80 = 240{,}000$$

6. A Jupiter year is almost 12 Earth years long. Since our year is 365 days, how many Earth days are there in a Jupiter year?

$$12 \times 365 = 4{,}380$$

7. 9 years after Voyager I was launched, it passed Neptune. Voyager I traveled nearly 280 million miles per year. How far did Voyager I travel to get to Neptune?

$$280{,}000{,}000 \times 9 = 2{,}520{,}000{,}000$$

About the book . . .

This book contains activity pages on such math topics as time, money, measurement and graphing, plus story problems with humorous twists and logical approaches to help students solve each one.

Credits . . .

Authors: Jan Kennedy, Paula Corbett, James E. Davidson, Ph.D., Robert W. Smith
Editors: Jackie Servis and Rhonda DeWaard
Artists: Jan Vonk, Karen Caminata, Pat Bakken, Cynthia Cutler, Bonnie Ann Gleason, Jim Price, Carol Tiernon
Production: Ann Dyer and Kurt Kemperman
Cover Photo: Dan Van Duinen